BACKCOUNTRY BETTY

CRAFTING WITH *Style*

BACKCOUNTRY BETTY

CRAFTING WITH *Style*

NATURE-INSPIRED PROJECTS

JENNIFER WORICK
ILLUSTRATED BY KATE QUINBY

SKIPSTONE

Published by Skipstone, an imprint of The Mountaineers Books
Manufactured in the United States of America

First printing 2009
12 11 10 09   5 4 3 2 1

Copy Editor: Kathleen Cubley
Cover Design: Kate Basart and Mayumi Thompson
Book Design and Layout: Mayumi Thompson
Cover and Interior Illustrations: Kate Quinby

Library of Congress Cataloging-in-Publication Data
Worick, Jennifer.
Backcountry Betty crafting with style : nature-inspired projects / by Jennifer Worick ; illustrated by Kate Quinby.
p. cm.
Includes bibliographical references and index.
ISBN 978-1-59485-139-1 (pbk. : alk. paper) 1. Nature craft. I. Title.
TT157.W6383 2009
745.5—dc22
2008051733

ISBN 13: 978-1-59485-139-1

Skipstone books may be purchased for corporate, educational, or other promotional sales. For special discounts and information, contact our Sales Department at 800-553-4453 or mbooks@mountaineersbooks.org.

Skipstone
1001 SW Klickitat Way
Suite 201
Seattle, Washington 98134
206.223.6303
www.skipstonepress.org
www.mountaineersbooks.org

Printed on recycled paper

LIVE LIFE. MAKE RIPPLES.

CONTENTS

To all my crafty friends, who provide me with inspiration every day

ACKNOWLEDGMENTS

For the past year or so, I've enjoyed my alter ego as Backcountry Betty. The original book (*Backcountry Betty: Roughing It in Style*) showed you how to navigate the wild with style and now, with *Backcountry Betty: Crafting with Style*, you'll learn how to create stylish crafts with materials from the wild. Coming up with inventive projects has not been a solo endeavor. I've had help, and lots of it.

For starters, I have to thank all the folks at The Mountaineers Books: my lovely editor Dana Youlin, Editor-in-Chief Kate Rogers, cute-as-a-button illustrator Kate Quinby, publicists Shanna Knowlton and Ashley Knecht, copy editor Kathleen Cubley, designers Kate Basart and Mayumi Thompson, and the entire staff who has always believed in the mission of Backcountry Betty.

My life coach (and avid knitter) Elizabeth Hechtman has been invaluable in helping me grow my career and my life, and my agent Joy Tutela with David Black Literary Agency has been both a fierce advocate and a friend.

Then there are my crafty friends and family members, who never fail to step up to the plate and help a Betty out: CraftStylish.com's Michaela Murphy; Spa Scotta owner Jessica Campbell; Odessa Herbals' creator Emily Mitchell; Darcey Howard, the chic force behind LifeStyled; my college roommate Maria Young; jewelry designer and pottery artist Evelyn Taylor; sewing instructor Cheryl Kuczek of Paradiso Designs; Sandra Watson of Go2Girl Events and Bridetiquette; Hilltop Yarn owner Jennifer Hill; The Make Shop & Studio owner Julie McCullough Kim; Alison Rooney; Kim Pavlek; Sacha Adorno; Melissa Wagner; Carilyn Platt; and all of my online Betty buddies.

I have to give props to my family, all of whom have mad skills befitting a crafty Betty: my woodworking fool of an uncle, Greg Hamlin; my dad Willis, who knows his way around a Dremel tool and a soldering gun; my brother John, who reminded me how to drill holes in those darn oyster shells Mom brought home after her shift at the Holiday Inn; and, of course, my mom for instilling early on a deep love for crafts and kitsch.

INTRODUCTION

We Backcountry Betties are seriously crafty gals. Not only do we know how to kick the outdoors', uh, butt, we also know our way around craft wire, knitting needles, and sewing machines. And you should see us with a hot glue gun.

The varied projects in this book speak to the adventurous nature of Backcountry Betty. Each project uses a found object from nature or our urban habitat and, through the power of your imagination and a few store-bought tools and materials, transforms that natural element into a clever, eye-catching craft.

Backcountry Betty: Crafting with Style adheres to and promotes a respectful environmental ethic. No materials should be taken from the outdoors unless they are downed items. That is, don't pull leaves off trees, don't cut down a sapling, don't grab a birds' nest if it's occupied. Get the picture? Pinecone on tree = bad. Pinecone on ground = future candle holder.

See, what sets this craft book apart from the rest (aside from the sassy, insightful writing, naturally) is its emphasis on the environment and how every Betty can bring those natural elements into projects both funky and elegant.

And I'll be with you every step of the way, providing clear, step-by-step instructions so Betties with two left thumbs won't feel intimidated or overwhelmed. Your innate Betty style will make up for any craft shortcomings you may have!

Each chapter, arranged by backcountry or backyard area, will feature projects using found items, including several "Lickety Split" projects that can be worked up in a jiff. With many of the projects, I've included additional suggestions for altering a project to your taste and purpose. That's what crafty Betties are all about, after all: customizing their works of art to their own personal (i.e. impeccable) style, and, with wit and expertise, putting their own twist on things. And if you aren't quite there with the "expertise" part, just fake it 'til you make it . . . and wear safety glasses!

Let's get crafting with style!

Chapter 1

STOCKING THE CRAFT PANTRY

Some of the easy-peasy projects won't require any additional materials, but the more ingenious (dare I say, impressive?) projects will, so I think it best to put together a "craft pantry," a list of materials—both of the natural and unnatural kind—every crafty Betty should keep on hand for when inspiration strikes.

CRAFT SUPPLIES TO PICK UP IN A CIVILIZED AREA

- artist wire in a medium gauge, such as 18 gauge
- base metal ball chain (the kind used for dog tags) with connector clasps
- base metal or sterling silver jump rings
- cardboard (break down those boxes from REI and eBay and reuse them)
- chain-nose pliers
- compass (the kind that draws a circle, not the kind you use to find yourself)
- construction paper
- craft glue
- cutting mat
- Dremel tool
- florist's foam
- hot glue gun
- Mod Podge Matte-Mat sealant, or similar type of clear sealant
- old newspapers and magazines
- plastic tarp or old shower curtain
- sharp scissors or X-Acto knife
- Sharpie markers
- small foam and bristle paintbrushes

Found Objects

Below are just a few ideas on what kind of found objects crafty Betties should collect during their wanderings. Keep your eyes peeled; you never know when you're going to spot the perfect pinecone, or a twisted twig that couldn't be more artistic if it tried.

Think about the times when you'll be more likely to find downed items—branches aplenty after a windstorm, or beach glass after the tide has gone out, for instance—and head out early in the morning to hunt and gather. After all, you won't be the only Betty on the prowl for earthy materials.

Into the Woods

- bark
- berries
- feathers
- leaves
- logs
- pinecones
- pine needles
- rocks
- sticks and branches
- vines

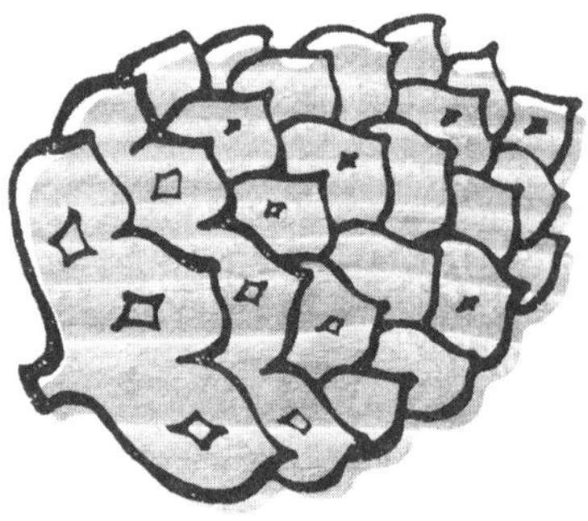

At the Shore

- beach glass
- driftwood
- grasses
- feathers
- flotsam (such as seaweed, ship wreckage, and gold doubloons)
- rocks
- sand
- shells

In the Meadow

- berries
- birds' nests
- cattails
- feathers
- grasses
- herbs
- pussy willows
- wheat stalks

In Your Own Backyard

- berries
- birds' nests
- feathers
- flowers
- gourds
- herbs
- leaves
- sticks
- vines

In the Urban Jungle

- aluminum cans
- cardboard coffee cozies
- CD jewel cases
- coffee stir sticks
- FedEx or USPS Tyvek bags
- glass bottles of all sizes
- medicine bottles
- paper coffee cups
- patterned papers
- plastic milk jugs
- plastic takeout containers
- plastic water bottles
- playing cards
- spare change

THE STORAGE STORY

When you bring home your materials and you aren't quite ready to dive in with your glue gun and Mod Podge, carefully store your found treasures in an out-of-the-way place (feathers, birds' nests, and shells can prove as fragile as your last boyfriend's ego). In general, think dry, dark and slightly cool; extra closets are hard to come by, but consider giving up precious clothing storage for equally precious craft supply storage. Damp areas can mildew your items or attract unwanted visitors looking to feast on your materials.

Crafting Alfresco

If you fancy working your crafty magic outdoors, here are a few pointers:

- Lay down a light- and solid-colored blanket so you can see if you drop any supplies.
- Find a level, ample work surface. The top of a large cooler could work, as long as no one needs to grab a frosty beer or snacklet.
- A sticky surface, velvet board, skillet, rimmed cookie sheet, or bead board with grooves will allow you to work without fear of losing materials to gravity or uneven ground.
- Think about what craft you want to take with you. Knitting is great, since you need only needles and yarn, while sewing or jewelry-making often requires notions and small findings that can be tricky to use in poor lighting, wind, or other less-than-optimal crafting conditions.
- Bring along Ziploc bags. They always come in handy for separating materials or toting works in progress.
- Pay attention to the wind. If it's blustery, avoid paint, Mod Podge, projects that use small or lightweight bits, or anything else that can become a big mess in a hot second.

Chapter 2

INTO THE WOODS

When you think of Backcountry Betty, you naturally think of her trekking through a forest, navigating switchbacks with ease, and breathing in the fresh, piney air. Sounds pretty great, doesn't it? The woods and wilderness are a particularly rich place to collect gorgeous natural items for craft projects. Don't even get me started on the pinecone.

When I go anywhere near a woody area (yes, the stand of trees near the zoo counts), I first breathe in the glorious air and look for any bald eagles perched in the uppermost branches of the highest tree. That takes about five seconds. Then I direct my attention downward, looking for treasures nestled amongst the pine needles and loamy ground. I have learned to bring along an extra Ziploc bag to collect pinecones, twigs, an interesting rock or two, feathers, and any other of nature's castoffs that can be transformed into an homage to the outdoors when incorporated into a craft project. I just make sure to delouse the item. Termites and bark beetles don't make for ideal craft materials (but believe me, I've thought about it).

PINECONE ROOM DIFFUSER

I love the smell of fresh pine. Breathing in the clean, woodsy air is my favorite part about hiking in the woods. I look forward to the holidays each year for various reasons, but mainly because I always buy up the yummy pine candles that seem to sprout up at all the fancy-pants gift shops.

I got to thinking that there must be a way to indulge my love of all things pine in my home year-round without having to hoard those holiday candles. I pulled out a few ingredients and in short order I had made an inexpensive room diffuser that also doubles as a pinecone bouquet. Who needs fresh flowers when you have the glorious pinecone at hand?

You'll need:

- large pot
- water
- tongs
- glass bottle with a small mouth (look for a pretty, vintage medicine bottle or a balsamic vinegar bottle, for instance)
- ½ cup carrier oil, such as sweet almond, jojoba, or extra-virgin olive oil
- 1 tablespoon essential oil of your choosing (may I suggest cedar or sandalwood?)
- 80-grade sandpaper
- 10 bamboo skewers
- hammer
- 10 small pinecones
- baking pan
- water
- Dremel tool with #561 multipurpose bit (looks like a drill bit)

Step 1: Fill a pot with water and bring to a boil. Using tongs, dip your bottle in the hot water bath for about ten minutes and set it aside to air dry. This will sterilize your bottle.

Working with Essential Oils

- ✧ Never apply essential oil directly to the skin.
- ✧ Look at the properties of each oil before using.
- ✧ Conduct a patch test if you are adding a new essential oil to a product, or if you have skin sensitivities or allergies.
- ✧ Keep essential oils away from pregnant women and small children.

Step 2: Mix the carrier oil (an oil that you can use to diffuse essential oils and other strong ingredients) and essential oil (take care never to apply directly to skin) in a measuring cup and pour into the sterilized bottle.

Step 3: With 80-grade sandpaper, roughen up each skewer to create a more porous surface. With a hammer, smash the pointed end of each skewer. Coat each skewer with the scented oil, place in the bottle, and set aside.

Step 4: Wet your pinecones in a baking pan filled with water. With your Dremel tool, drill a small hole in the center of the bottom of a pinecone, about 1/4 inch deep, resubmerging the pinecone if it starts to smoke. You can drill the pinecone while it is submerged, but be careful to only insert the drill bit, not any other part of the Dremel tool, into the water.

Step 5: Slip the drilled pinecone onto the flat end of one of the oil-coated bamboo skewers and place the skewer back in the bottle. Repeat for the rest of the pinecones. The pinecones should sit snugly on each skewer. (Gluing them may prevent the oil from traveling up the skewer onto the pinecone.) Wait for one to two days for the scent to start disseminating into the room. If the smell isn't strong enough for your liking, place a drop or two of the essential oil on each pinecone. Smells almost as good as breathing in the great outdoors, doesn't it?

PINE NEEDLE SACHET

It's well documented that I love, love, love the smell of fresh pine (don't all Betties?). I keep the scent going year-round with adorable little sachets made with old handkerchiefs. Tuck these little beauties into drawers and give them as sweet hostess gifts and party favors to other like-nosed Betties.

You'll need:

- 1 cup pine needles
- mortar and pestle
- iron
- 1 vintage handkerchief (about 14 x 14 inches)
- tailor's chalk or erasable fabric marker
- sharp scissors
- pins
- thread (polyester or a cotton-poly blend)
- needle
- large button

Step 1: Check that your pine needles aren't attached to any cones and that they don't have any residual stickiness on them. If you have time, let them dry out for a week or two. Break up the needles a bit if they are particularly long, place them in a mortar or bowl, and grind them with the pestle. Set aside.

Step 2: Iron your handkerchief and lay it on a flat surface, wrong side up. Divide it into four squares with tailor's chalk. Using sharp scissors cut out one square from your hankie. Set the rest aside for later use.

Step 3: Lay out your fabric, wrong side up.

Step 3

(If it's a plain white handkerchief rather than a patterned one, consider using fabric paint and stenciling or stamping pinecones and trees on the right side. If you do this, wait for the paint to dry thoroughly before sewing.) Fold each end toward the middle so that all four points are touching. Imagine that you're making a cootie catcher/ fortuneteller thingie, but out of fabric instead of paper. Pin the adjoining sides to each other.

Step 4: Thread your needle, leaving a tail of about 2 feet, knotting the threads together a couple of inches from the ends. Starting at one end of the hankie and working toward the middle, pull the thread through the two pieces about 1/8 inch from the edge, pulling until the knot touches the fabric. To keep all the piney goodness inside your sachet, you'll need to use a backstitch for your seams. Pass the needle back through the fabric about 1/4 inch away

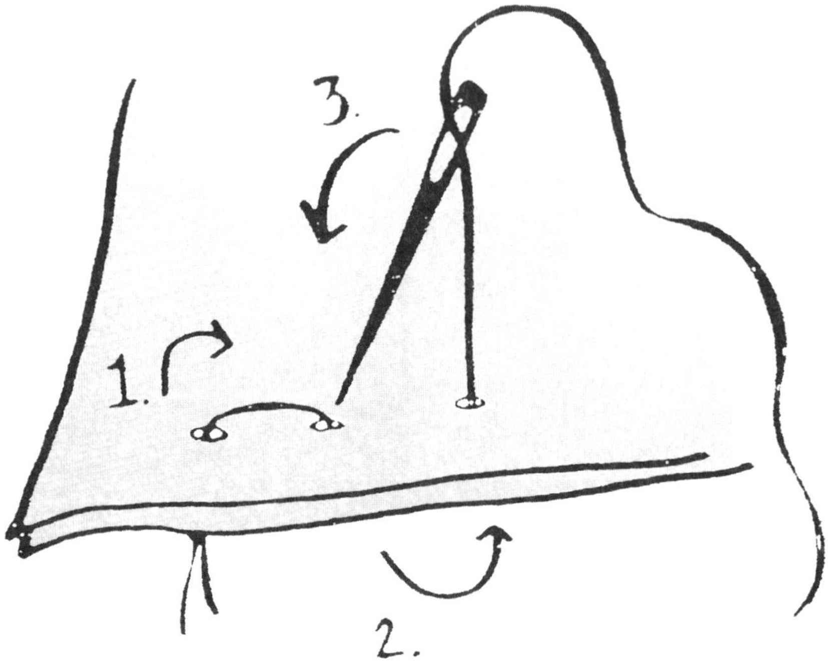

Step 4

from the first hole, while maintaining a 1/8-inch seam allowance. There should be a 1/4-inch gap between your first stitch and your needle. You need to close the gap to create a seamless line of stitches. Pass the needle into the fabric right next to (or even into the actual hole of) your first stitch. Now, sort of jumping over the second hole, make another 1/4-inch stitch, backtrack and pass your needle into or next to the second hole you made and come back through the fabric. Can you see what's going on? You have a continuous line of thread. Continue in this manner until you reach the center. Now, using the same thread, stitch together another two adjoining sides, starting from the center and working your way to the ends. Cut your thread and knot the ends together close to the fabric.

Step 5: Repeat step 4 for the remaining two sides, stopping 2 inches from the final end. Turn your hankie inside out, pulling the right side through the hole. Fill your handkerchief with the crushed pine needles and finish stitching the sides together with a tiny backstitch.

Step 6: Finish off your sachet by threading a needle and sewing a button to the center of the sachet (where all four points meet). Pass through the top and bottom layers of fabric to give your sachet a bit of a cushioned look. That's it! Pop it in a drawer or closet and enjoy.

Note: To amp up the scent of the sachet, add a few drops of pine essential oil to the needles, or add a couple of tablespoons of dried lavender buds to the mix.

DOG PARK PILLOW

Are you sick of your car getting mucked up and smelling like wet fur? Well, help is at hand in the form of this hot-diggety dog bed. Cedar chips and lavender will neutralize odor and repel fleas, while a pillow cover—made out of old but absorbent bath towels—can be thrown in the wash after your pooch leaves his mark.

You'll need:

- 2 old bath towels
- pins
- sewing machine
- thread (cotton or cotton-poly blend)
- 6 large snaps
- 1 old, king-sized pillowcase
- 1 bushel cedar chips (if you're unable to find some downed cedar to chip up, you can also use a large bag of cedar chip cat litter)
- 1 or 2 cups crushed lavender buds

Step 1: Place the two towels, right sides facing, on a flat surface and pin them together. Sew three sides together with a ½-inch seam allowance, leaving one short end open. Turn right side out. Sew six large snaps along the open short edge, about 1 inch from the edge. Set aside.

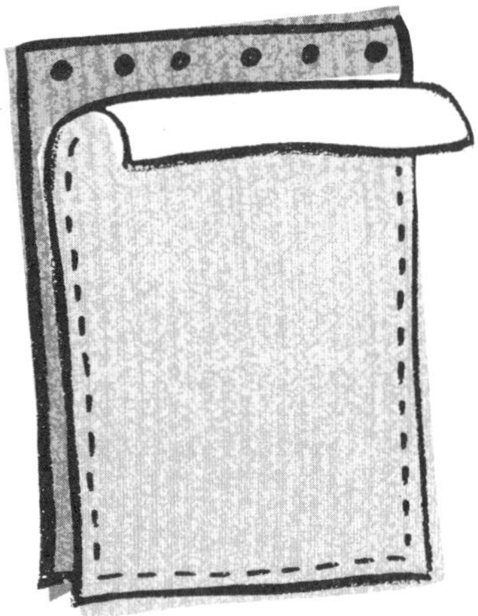

Step 1

Step 2: Stuff the pillowcase with cedar chips and lavender until plump but not overstuffed. Following the seam of the pillowcase opening, sew the pillowcase shut with a small, sturdy stitch (if hand sewing, see page 19 for information on backstitching).

Step 3: Place the stuffed, sealed pillowcase in the towel cover and snap the towel shut. Place the pillow on the back seat of your car and guide your pooch to it when traveling to and from the dog park. When the towel cover gets soiled, simply unsnap it and throw it in the wash.

The Pinecone Zone

Everyone knows what a pinecone looks like, right? Well, sort of. While working up the projects for this book, my obsession with pinecones kicked into high gear. Before long, my place was lousy with pinecones of every shape and size. I have a couple of ginormous cones from a sugar pine as well as little clusters of cones still on their branches. My favorite pinecone, however, is rather flat and, in the palm, looks like a blooming rose. How gorgeous is that? The possibilities for pinecones may not be limitless, but they are many. Here are a few ideas.

- Use cone "petals" as shingles for a dollhouse.
- Collect and place pinecones in a pretty basket to give as a firestarter kit. Dipping them repeatedly in paraffin makes them even better tinder for a fire. You can even sprinkle a few drops of pine essential oil to scent the room prior to use. Make a gift tag with instructions for use and draw or stamp a pinecone on it.
- Wrap wire around a few top petals and create a hook. Instant tree ornament. Add glitter glue to the petals' tips for an even more festive look.
- Use whole pinecones as placecard holders for a dinner party.
- Line a shelf or a tabletop with pinecones for a quick and elegant room accent.

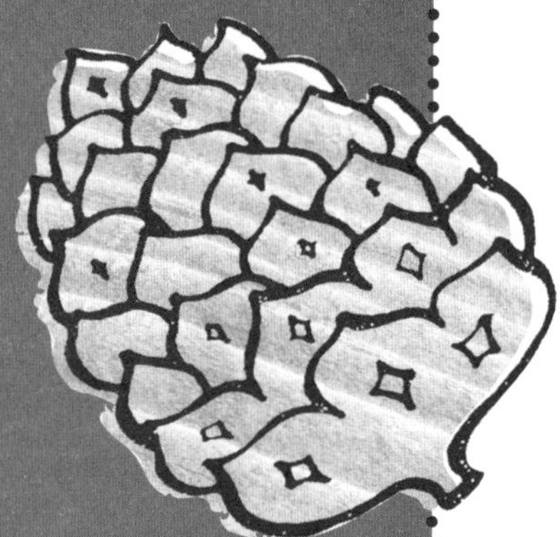

PINECONE-PETAL PIN

I like flair, both in the general sense and in the specific way of tricking yourself out with interesting pins. Don't get me wrong; I don't load up suspenders with pins of Rick Springfield or kitties hanging from tree limbs urging me to "Hang in there." No, I like sparkly vintage brooches and handmade knitted or felt pins, and for a signature look I usually pin one on a coat.

Recently, while staring at my collection of pinecones, I visualized a pin made out of the individual "petals" of pinecones. When you lay out the petals in a circle and layer them over each other, you can quickly create a flower-shaped pin, perfect for sprucing up an old coat or a fleece vest.

You'll need:

- 1 gorgeous pinecone
- wood-carving knife
- 4 x 4 inch square of vinyl, suede, or sturdy felt
- compass
- fabric marker
- sharp scissors
- hot glue gun
- acorn top or cloth-covered button
- 1-inch-wide pinback

Step 1: Deconstruct the pinecone by carefully pulling off the petals, starting in the middle and working your way to the top (the bottom petals are often very rigid and sort of meshed together rather than distinct, fully-formed petals). I like to try to snap them at the base and then wiggle them to the right and left until they disengage from the cone. If they

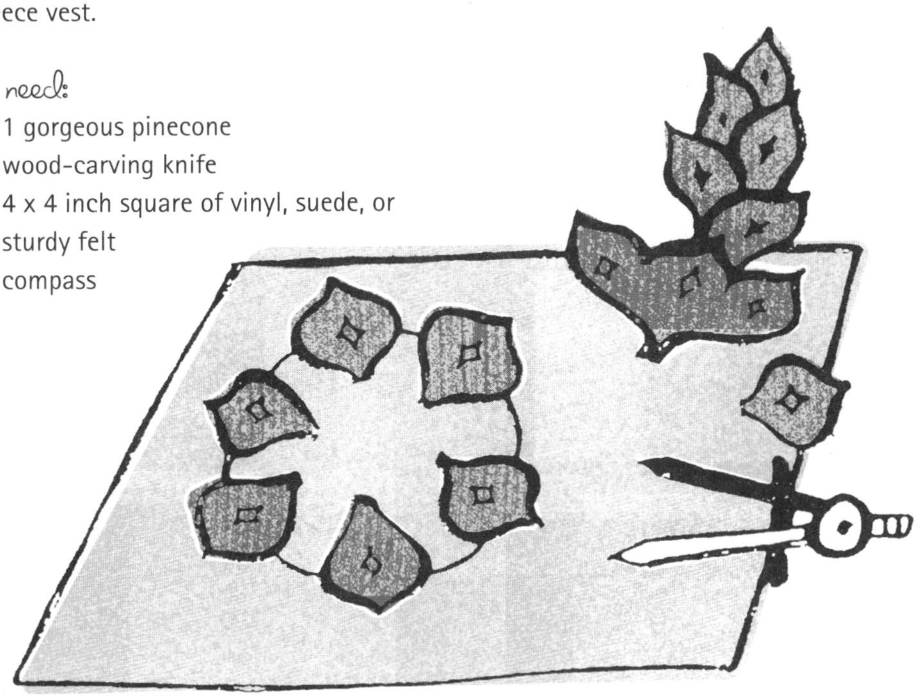

Step 2

won't come off easily, use a wood-carving knife to carefully saw off each petal as close to the core as possible.

Step 2: Lay out the largest petals in a circle and measure the diameter. Using a compass fitted with a fabric marker, trace the circle onto the back of your vinyl and carefully cut out the circle.

Step 3: With a hot glue gun, place a dollop of glue on the back side of each petal and glue each piece to the vinyl until you have a circle of petals. Let the glue cool thoroughly. Now add a second layer atop the first, taking care to place glue only on the new petals where they will touch the base layer. Let the glue cool again. Now, glue an acorn top (or a button) in the center of your pinecone flower.

Step 4: When the glue is cool, carefully add a pinback to your creation by gluing the pinback bar to the back of the vinyl. Place the pinback toward the top of the pin, rather than in the center, to prevent the pin from flopping over when worn. Let the glue cool and wear your pin with careful pride.

Note: This is a fragile pin, so be careful when wearing it on a jacket or shirt. A handbag slung over the shoulder could easily crush your handiwork. Consider pinning or gluing the flower to the top of an ornamental box or backing it with cardstock and placing it in a shadow box.

SEEDPOD SHADOW BOX

As a kid, I was fascinated by maple seedpods, which when they fell from the tree (or my hand) would spin around as they fell to Earth. We called them whirligigs. When my college roommate Maria sent me a bag of these little guys, I was thrilled. They are still magical to me so I wanted to showcase them. I got a hold of a cheap shadow box from one of those superstores that are suddenly supercool and tried to recapture the motion of this natural wonder.

You'll need:

- 8 to 10 maple seedpods
- X-Acto knife
- foam brush
- Mod Podge Matte-Mat
- 8 x 10 inch black shadow box
- 1 sheet of white 8½ x 11 inch cardstock
- 1 sheet of brown 8½ x 11 inch cardstock
- scissors
- double-sided tape
- 1/16-inch-thick foam tape dots

Step 1

Step 1: Lay out your design, fanning the seedpods out so they look like they're in motion, spinning. The pods themselves are a bit bulky so trim down all the bottom ones, carefully removing the seedpod with an X-Acto knife. Remove the pods from the same side on each whirligig so they will fan out in the same direction. Leave one seedpod intact (this is the one that will be on top).

Step 2: Now it's time to preserve these little beauties so they'll hold up in the shadow box. I like to coat them, using a foam brush, with Mod Podge Matte-Mat. Coat the backside first and let dry. Turn them over and repeat the process; let dry.

Step 3: Remove the back of the shadow box and trace the outline onto a piece of white cardstock. With scissors, cut cardstock to fit and, using double-sided tape, affix the cardstock to the back of the shadow box. Set aside.

Step 4: Cut the brown cardstock to 5 x 5 inches. This is your mounting background for the whirligigs. Lay out the first pod, taping it

Step 5

to the cardstock with two or three foam dots. Place a foam dot close to the center of the pod and carefully position your second pod on top of the first. The center of the second pod should be aligned with the first pod, with the end of the whirligig fanning away from the end of the first pod. Continue placing pods in this manner until you've completed a circle.

Step 5: Affix foam dots to the corners and center of the back of the brown cardstock and position it in the middle of the white backing. Put your shadow box together and enjoy the wonder of the whirligig all year long.

Note: You can use this shadow box technique with a variety of items, including pressed flowers or leaves.

FRAME JOB

My mom has this awesome lamp that has traveled from home to home and room to room. It was a gift from my Uncle Greg, a serious woodworker. He made a base out of a slice of birch wood and then made a lampshade out of birch bark. It has held up surprisingly well over the years and it looks charming in my mom's rustic farmhouse. I asked Uncle Greg to reveal his trade secrets and the result is this bark-covered frame that will bring a little cabin style into your home.

You'll need:

- 20 to 30 pieces of seasoned (completely dry) birch bark
- large pair of scissors or a utility knife
- 8 x 10 inch frame, or mirror with at least a 2-inch-wide flat frame
- hot glue gun
- art or photo to frame

Step 1: Rip up the bark or cut it with a large pair of scissors or a utility knife. I like a more

Step 2

rustic look so I just rip the pieces into rough squares and rectangles.

Step 2: Before attaching the pieces, lay them out on the frame to get an idea of the design. Pretend you are shingling your frame, overlapping the pieces slightly. Now set the bark pieces aside in the order you want to use them. With a hot glue gun, apply glue to the top edge of your bark, and affix it to the frame, starting from the bottom and working your way up to the top of the frame. Let the glue cool (which should take only minutes).

Step 3: Place your art or photo in the frame and secure the back. Hang and admire your handiwork.

NOTES

- ✧ If you want to take bark straight from birch wood, make sure the wood is seasoned before you remove the bark. Just stack the wood in a dry spot and let it season for a year, and then peel off the bark. Or, if you are scampering in the woods and spy a dead, downed tree, you can pull the bark off the tree pretty easily. Let the bark dry thoroughly, however, before using it in your project.
- ✧ You can also affix birch bark to a lampshade or birdhouse.
- ✧ In lieu of birch bark, you can use pinecone "petals" for your material. Just choose a small frame or other surface to cover, as the petals will be smaller than the bark (unless you find a few ginormous pinecones).

Lickety Split: "Gold" Leafing Leaves

Clean stems, branches, and leaves of beech or birch. Place the branches in a bottle or vase filled with a mix of one part liquid glycerin and two parts hot water. Keep in a dark cool place for two to three weeks, wiping the leaves occasionally with the mixture to keep them from drying out. The absorption process is complete when all the leaves have turned a uniform color. Foliage will take on a rich gold or dark color and can be used in a dried flower arrangement or on a wreath.

GEM BRANCH

Living in a small space, I am always challenged when it comes to storage. Shoes are put in plastic boxes and stacked up in columns twelve boxes high, yarn is squirreled away under my bed and in my linen closet. Then there's my jewelry. Necklaces hang off towel racks in the bathroom, rings are tucked away in boxes, earrings are displayed on a mesh frame. But for my ever-growing jewelry collection, these storage solutions are woefully inadequate. After all, we Betties are always making new things with which to adorn ourselves.

So I turn to the outdoors for a little help with my jewelry storage issues. A few branches picked up in your wanderings can quickly become lovely organic displays for your baubles. Walk through your neighborhood or a wooded area after a fierce storm and look for downed branches with lots of offshoots, the twistier the better. If the branch is already hard and dry, letting it dry for a couple of days is probably sufficient; if it's still green, you'll have to wait until it is completely seasoned.

You'll need:

- downed, twisty branch, seasoned
- 80-grade sandpaper
- spray paint and newspaper, optional
- vase
- sand or rocks (amount depends on your vase and branch size)

Step 1: Dry out your branch. When it is completely seasoned (depending on the thickness of your branch, seasoning could take several months), smooth the surface with sandpaper.

Step 2: If you want to glam up your branch display, put newspaper down outdoors and spray paint the branch in the color of your choice. Let dry, and spray the other side of the branch. Let dry.

Step 3: Place your branch in a vase and fill in around it with sand or small rocks (you could also use beach glass or marbles) to hold it upright. Now simply drape the offshoots with your favorite necklaces, bracelets, earrings, and rings. This display is so lovely you may want to consider showcasing it in your bedroom or living room.

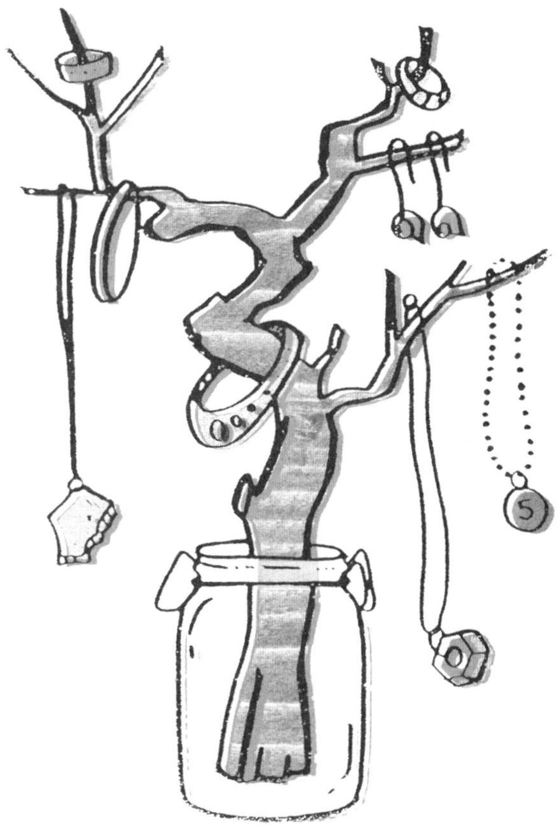

JIGSAW PUZZLE

I have a love/hate relationship with jigsaw puzzles. Just like Scrabble and crossword puzzles, I usually steer clear of them because I become downright obsessed. I can't quit until I tuck the last pesky piece into its snug place. I once visited the Hamptons with some friends and, instead of trolling for shells or celebrities, I sat in the living room at a card table for what seemed like the entire weekend mulling over a huge puzzle of the Grand Canyon. I figured it would be nice to set others on this obsessive gaming path by whipping up a truly unique puzzle, made from your own photography or artwork.

You'll need:

- 120-grade sandpaper
- flat 8 x 10 inch piece of basswood or pine, 1 inch thick
- computer and printer
- favorite digital photo of a tree, pinecone, or nature scene
- Sharpie marker
- tape
- 2 sheets of carbon paper, one dark and one white if possible
- stylus or pencil
- set of acrylic paints
- paint brushes in various sizes
- parchment paper
- safety glasses
- electric jigsaw
- newspapers
- satin polyurethane spray varnish

Step 1: Sand all sides of the wood until smooth. Set aside.

Step 2: Select a photo and, using your computer's photo software, increase the contrast of the image so the light and dark areas are very prominent. Size the image to 8 x 10 inches and print it out.

Step 3: With a Sharpie or thick marker, trace over the main lines of your image. Basically, you want to create strong, graphic lines so you can paint your image easily onto the wood. Tape a sheet of carbon paper (carbon side facing the wood) to the surface of the wood. Tape your photo on top of the carbon paper. With a stylus or pencil (you need a hard point for tracing), trace over the lines you created on your image, transferring the carbon onto the wood.

Step 4: With your acrylic paints and a small brush, paint your biggest and darkest areas first, allowing each layer to dry before moving onto the next color (if colors are touching or overlapping). As the final step, add details and shading with a smaller brush. Clean your brushes and let the paint dry.

Step 5: To make the puzzle, draw an 8 x 10 inch rectangle on parchment paper. Draw wiggly and curving lines in your rectangle to create large puzzle pieces. If you want, try creating traditional puzzle pieces (that sort of have a lock-and-key configuration with a rounded tab fitting into a gap in the next piece). Now tape a piece of carbon paper (white if possible) facedown on your artwork (tape the piece to the

Step 3

unpainted sides so you don't pull any paint up). Tape the puzzle design on top of the carbon and trace the lines so the carbon is transferred onto the wood.

Note: You could also try using chalk to draw a freeform puzzle design on the painted wood.

Step 6: Put on your safety glasses and find a safe, roomy workspace. With a jigsaw, carefully cut out the puzzle pieces, keeping fingers far from the blade. Work from one end of the piece of wood to the other and keep the saw on a low setting at a 90-degree angle to the wood while working. (You will have a lot of sawdust as well, so if it's possible, do this outside or on a surface that's easy to sweep up.) When the puzzle is completely cut out, sand the rough edges of the pieces. Lay out the pieces on newspaper in a ventilated space (like outside) and spray them with a clear lacquer, such as Deft brand, to finish. Let dry completely and enjoy!

Lickety Split: Rock Spa

Large river rocks are great tools for body treatments. Cool them down in the fridge and place one in the center spot between your eyes for sinus relief or place one over each eye to relieve puffiness. Heat rocks in a Crock-Pot full of water and treat your tight muscles to a hot stone massage. Better yet, get someone else to rock your world and rub you down.

Step 5

IT'S A SIGN

A lot of my ideas for outdoor crafts stem from my childhood. As a tomboy, I sort of shadowed my two older brothers at a distance so I wouldn't hurt their street cred (which is hilarious, seeing as we lived on a road in farm country very few cars ever thought to traverse). Anyway, I watched them as they dabbled with "manly" crafts—you know, stuff involving leather, wood, knives, and tools that could maim or burn.

I was entranced.

To that end, I whipped out my trusty wood-burning tool to make a cool sign so everyone who knocks on my door knows that they are about to experience "Camp Betty."

You'll need:

- 150-grade sandpaper
- piece of scrap wood (of the same type as your project wood)
- approximately 10 x 12 inch flat piece of soft wood, such as bass or pine
- pencil
- wood-burning tool with different tips
- newspapers
- satin polyurethane spray varnish, such as Deft brand
- foam brush
- 2 small nail and screw sawtooth hangers
- hammer or screwdriver

Step 1: Using 150-grade sandpaper, sand all sides of your wood (both your scrap wood and your project piece) until smooth.

Step 2: Take your wood-burning tool for a test drive. Plug it in and let it heat up (take care, these tools can heat up to more than 900°F). Grab a pencil and lightly sketch a simple design or phrase on your practice scrap. Now, holding your tool like a pencil, make a few strokes to get a feel for it and to see how the wood reacts to it. Swap out the

Step 2

Step 3

tips—making sure to cool the tool between uses—and experiment with different line shapes and thicknesses. Cool, huh?

Step 3: When you're ready, use a pencil to lightly print "Camp Betty" (or your chosen phrase) on your project wood, carefully spacing letters out or being more freeform in your approach. Add an acorn, leaf, or pinecone for an additional Betty flourish. Now use the wood-burning tool to go over the lines. Unplug your tool and move on to the final step.

Step 4: For rich color and a long-lasting sign, you'll need to varnish your sign. Lay down newspapers in a well-ventilated area and spray several coats of varnish on your door plaque, letting it dry between coats and cleaning up any streaks or drips with a small foam brush.

Step 5: In each top corner of your sign, nail or screw in a sawtooth picture hanger. You're ready to announce to the world—or at least to the UPS man—that Camp Betty is open for business.

LOG CABIN CANDLE

You may not have the pleasure of living in a log cabin, but you can bring a little of that rustic charm into your home by creating a votive candle holder out of downed birch. Living in an apartment in the big city, it's the best I can do until I can scamper to a rental in the woods. And with a pine-scented candle popped in the votive holder, I can close my eyes and channel my inner Betty. No sweat.

You'll need:

- newspapers
- safety glasses
- electric hand-drill with 9/64-inch or 11/64-inch bit
- 2 foot x 4 inch board, 3/4 inch thick
- round slice of pine or birch wood with bark still on, 4 inches in diameter, 3 inches tall
- #8 or #10 x 1 5/8-inch-long sheetrock screws
- screwdriver
- 2 1/4-inch Forstner bit
- 80-grade sandpaper
- clear glass votive holder
- votive candle

Step 1: Spread out the newspapers on your work surface (this will help collect sawdust and wood chips when you drill). First of all, you need to secure your future candle holder to a piece of wood to stabilize it while drilling. Put on your safety glasses. Drill four holes in a square 3 inches apart in the center of the board and do the same on one end of the slice of pine or birch. For a #8 screw, drill a 9/64-inch hole and for a #10 screw, drill an 11/64-inch hole. Fit the screws through the board and using a screwdriver, twist the screws into the holes in the bottom of the pine or birch wood. The board and screws act like a vise to keep the wood from spinning when you drill the hole in the top of your candle holder (there will be quite a bit of torque from the large Forstner bit).

Step 2: Keep those safety glasses on and secure your Forstner bit in the electric hand-drill. Step on the board and hold the drill between your legs, locking your elbows between your knees, which will give you much more stability when you drill the large round hole. Holding the drill at a 90-degree angle to the top of the wood, drill a hole that is 2 1/4 inches in circumference and 1 inch deep.

Step 3: Remove the screws and board from your candle holder. With the sandpaper, smooth the edges around the new hole and on the top of the wood. Pop a glass votive holder in the hole, add a candle, and enjoy soft candlelight in your home.

CARRYING A TORCH

With your Log Cabin Candle (see page 34), you can create a backyard torch. Consider lining an outside path with a whole row of these charming homemade torches for a rustic tiki touch.

You'll need:

- long, straight branch, 1 inch in diameter, 3 to 4 feet long
- pocket knife
- safety glasses
- 1 1/8-inch Forstner bit
- electric hand-drill
- Log Cabin Candle (see page 34)
- carpenter's wood glue

Step 1: Using a pocket knife, whittle one end of your branch into a point, using long, slow strokes. (Lay it on a work surface and cut away from your body.) This end will serve as your stake in the ground. The other end should have a flat, clean edge.

Step 2: Put on those safety glasses! Secure the Forstner bit in your drill. Turn the Log Cabin Candle upside down, place it on the ground, and brace it between your feet. (Bending over it and pushing down with the drill will give you maximum leverage.) Now drill a 1/2-inch hole in the bottom of the candle holder, making sure you have enough depth to do this so you don't drill all the way through to the votive hole on the top of the candle holder.

Fill the new hole with wood glue and place the flat end of the branch into it. If the branch doesn't quite fit, use your pocket knife to whittle the end of the branch until it fits snugly into the new hole. Keep the branch upright until the glue dries (anywhere from one to six hours; refer to the directions on the glue bottle). A hot, dry location will aid the drying process.

Step 3: When dry, turn over, insert the branch into the ground (well away from any foliage), add the glass votive and candle to the candle holder, and enjoy.

Note: If you don't have the energy to whip up a lot of Log Cabin Candles, you could cut one end of your long branch so that it's flat and use a hot glue gun to affix a glass votive holder to it.

Lickety Split: Nature's Candlesticks

Who needs a pair of crystal Tiffany candlesticks when you can make your own taper holders with a pair of nifty pinecones? With a screw, make a hole in the bottom of a taper candle. Remove the screw and then fit the candle onto the top "petal" of a large pinecone (make sure the pinecone has a flat, stable base to support the candle). Place on a tray or plate, light up, and let the candle drip elegantly onto the pinecone.

Chapter 3

AT THE SHORE

Who doesn't like long walks on the beach? No one, according to the many profiles I've cruised on Internet dating sites. I love the beach, too, partly because of all the wonderful memories I've made there. I've made out with my college boyfriend in the dunes (sand is *so* not sexy in reality). I've frolicked with my nieces in the surf of Lake Michigan. I've watched my dad grill up some Polish sausage at a family reunion. I've fallen asleep in a warm daze on the beaches of the Atlantic, only to be awakened by the exclamations of other beach-goers as they spied dolphins (or were they porpoises?) in the surf.

Though they all have sand, surf, and the smell of Coppertone, every beach is different. One has only to compare the red rocks streaked with white that my dad sent me straight from the shores of Lake Michigan with the black rocks of Vancouver's Kitsilano Beach. Growing up near Lake Michigan and now living in the Northwest, there's been ample opportunity for me to collect shells, rocks, sand, feathers, and driftwood. I've used my collection to concoct these beach-inspired projects.

CLAMDLES

Yeah, you heard me: clamdles! It's a clamshell, it's a candle, it's a clamdle! Marry your love of the ocean with your love of comforting candles by making a distinctive candle with your favorite natural fragrance and a shell from a memorable clambake. Add citronella or sandalwood oil if you plan on using these clamdles outside, as the oil acts as a natural insect repellent. And for added safety both in and out of doors, place the clamdles in sand to ensure that they remain level and upright. On a plate or in a bowl, they'll make a kick-ass centerpiece at your dinner party. Prepare to be admired.

You'll need:

- 2 1-inch wicks with tabs
- ½ cup soy-wax flakes
- double boiler (or glass measuring cup and saucepan)
- 2 large clamshell halves, cleaned and dried
- old dishtowel
- 20 drops essential oil of your choosing (I used half lemongrass, half orange blossom). (See *Working with Essential Oils*, page 18.)

Step 1: Straighten out the wicks and set aside.

Step 2: Heat the soy wax in a double boiler (or glass measuring cup inside a pan of boiling water) until it's completely melted.

Step 3: Place the shells on an old dishtowel, with the insides facing up. (The towel will stabilize the shells.) Add the essential oil to the melted wax and carefully pour it into the shells. Let cool for a few minutes and, while wax is still gooey, place the wick in the center of the shell. As the wax cools, it will leave a depression in the middle

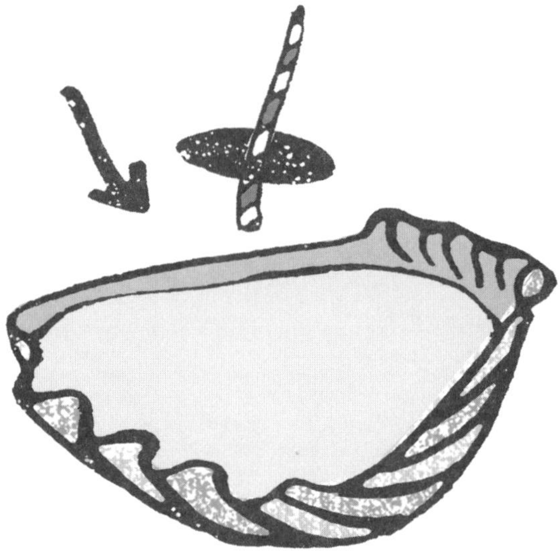

Step 3

of the clamdle so top off with some of the wax still in your double boiler. Let cool thoroughly.

Step 4: Light up!

Note: If you don't have the time to make a full-on clamdle, just put a dollop of wax or florist's putty in the inside of a shell and plop in a tea light. Not as impressive, but beautifully beachy nevertheless.

The Shell Station

Just as I find pinecones to be fruits of the forest, so too do I think shells are gifts from the sea. Their shapes are magical and I'm always stunned at how something so seemingly delicate can wind up intact in the surf. Mine is not to ask why, it's just to brush off the sand and find a way to showcase these natural wonders. Here are some quick ideas.

- Drill holes in shells—or look for shells with holes already in them—and make natural wind chimes.
- Clean found shells thoroughly (boil to sterilize) and use them as bowls for dip or nuts.
- Glue small shells around a frame to showcase your favorite beach photo.
- Use broken bits of shell in a mosaic tabletop or trivet.
- Turn a large clamshell into a soap dish.
- Drill a hole in two small, matching shells, add an earwire, and you've got a quick pair of summer earrings.

ROCK STAR PENDANT

One of the biggest thrills when walking along the beach (aside from frolicking in the surf with a buff companion, of course) is discovering that perfect rock amongst the flotsam and jetsam that washes up on shore. Rather than tucking your little gem away or throwing it in a bowl, show off your beach swag by making an organic pendant that conveys just how earthy and laid-back you are.

You'll need:

- measuring tape
- wire cutters
- chain-nose pliers
- 1 foot of 20-gauge wire (can be sterling silver, gold-filled, or artistic wire)
- round-nose pliers
- 1 gorgeous rock
- 2 feet waxed cotton, hemp, or leather cord
- jewelry cement, such as Bond 527 Multi-Purpose Cement
- 2 coil cord ends (2mm in metal of your choice)
- 2 split rings
- 1 lobster clasp

Step 1: Cut 12 inches of wire. (You may need more if your rock is large.) Measure 3 inches on one end of wire and, with your chain-nose pliers, bend the end at a 90-degree angle. Place your round-nose pliers close to the bend and wrap the short end of the wire around one end of the pliers, creating a loop. Wrap that end of the wire around the base of the loop twice. Clip off the remaining wire with your wire cutters and gently tuck the end in with the chain-nose pliers so it's flush with the rest of the wrapped wire. This wire loop is called the bail.

Step 2: With the long end of your wire, use a freeform approach to wrap your rock. Wrap the wire in several directions and around any outcroppings or depressions in the rock so you capture it snugly in a wire cage. End by bringing the wire up toward the bail. You want to have about an inch of wire left. Take the end of the wire in your chain-nose pliers and wrap it twice, as tightly as possible, around the base of your bail.

Step 2

Step 3: You can either cut the wire and tuck in the end so it's flush with the rest of the wrapped coil (as you did in step 1) or you can create a coiled vine. To do this, place the end of the wire toward the top of your round-nose pliers. Start turning the pliers so the wire coils around one side of the pliers. When you reach the base of the bail and run out of wire to coil, remove the pliers. With your chain-nose pliers, carefully grab the end of the coiled wire and pull it down away from the bail on the front side of the pendant. Tuck the end under one of the wires that is wrapped around the stone. The pendant is done! Doesn't it look cool? Don't you want to wear it? Well, you need to put it on a cord, first.

Note: If the wire cage around the stone seems loose, turn the pendant over so the back is facing you. With your chain-nose pliers, grasp one of the loose wires and gently twist it so the wire becomes taut. Don't twist more than 90 degrees or you risk breaking the wire.

Step 3

Step 4: Thread your pendant onto the cord and hold it up around your neck to estimate the length that you want your pendant, leaving 1/4 to 1/2 inch for the clasp. So if you want a 16-inch pendant, cut the cord to 15½ inches. (If you want a more casual and feminine look, don't bother with a clasp at all and just tie the ends of a longer cord tightly in a bow to secure the pendant around your neck.)

Step 5: Hold up your cord and apply a dab of glue to the end. Thread a coil cord end onto the gluey end. With your chain-nose pliers, push on the bottom of the coil so that it presses snugly against the cord, securing it. Slip your pendant onto the cord and repeat the coil process on the other end of the cord.

Step 6: Twist open the end of your coil cord end with the chain-nose pliers. Slip the split ring onto the loop and close the coil cord end. With a fingernail or your chain-nose pliers, open up an end of the second split ring and slip the end of a lobster clasp onto it. Now pry open the other coil cord end and attach the clasp by slipping the split ring to the coil end. Close the coil end and that's it! You now have a lovely accessory to break out at the beach or bistro.

Note: For a more elegant look, consider using a chain for your pendant, or a braided hemp cord for an even more organic feel. You can even braid together three different cords. Just make sure the bail is large enough to accommodate the three strands.

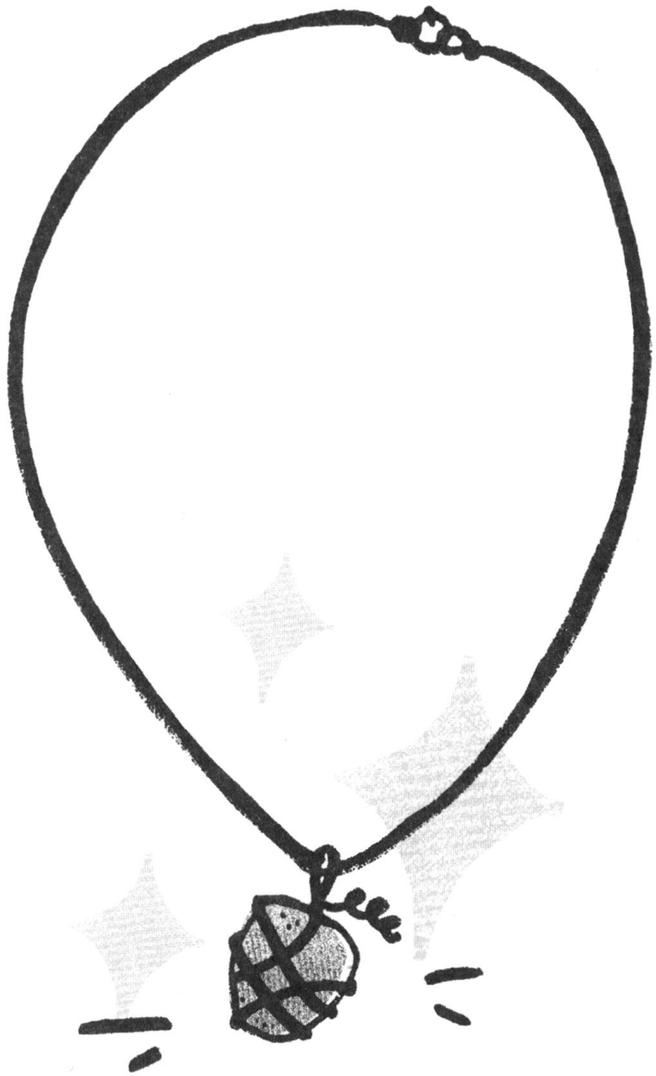

THE MOBILE HOME

I love mobiles. I had one when I was a preteen Betty. Fish made out of ribbons danced and swayed in the air as the dulcet tones of Leif Garrett wafted through my bedroom. More recently, I've enjoyed looking at kinetic Calder pieces at various museums and cheap mobiles tacked into the ceiling at the dentist's office, and I've busted out my collection of beach glass to make a lovely, organic mobile, perfect for summer or to give as a hostess gift when visiting a friend's seaside cottage.

You'll need:

- safety glasses
- old kitchen sponge with a rough side
- shallow metal pan
- water
- 30 to 40 pieces of beach glass
- Dremel tool with 1/16-inch diamond drill bit and #561 multipurpose drill bit
- cleaning stone for Dremel diamond bits
- scissors
- sturdy fishing line or Illusion Cord
- strong glue such as Superglue or E6000
- pen and paper
- 10 pieces of driftwood
- Sharpie marker
- 1-inch key ring or large split ring
- awl or pin

Step 1: Don some oh-so-attractive safety glasses. Place a sponge rough-side-up in a shallow pan of water. Place pieces of beach glass on the sponge. To drill holes in the glass pieces, place your Dremel tool with the diamond bit at a 90-degree angle to the glass. Position the hole about 1/8 inch from an edge of the glass. Set your Dremel tool on low and don't press too hard; the Dremel will do the work for you. Increase the speed as you get more comfortable with drilling. You'll know when the hole is made as there will be a moment with no resistance. And keep the glass and the area you are drilling damp. You may need to press down on the sponge every so often to keep it wet. Clean the drill bit after every few holes drilled. (Set the Dremel to the lowest speed and gently hold the cleaning stone to the edge and tip of your diamond bit, keeping both in the water.)

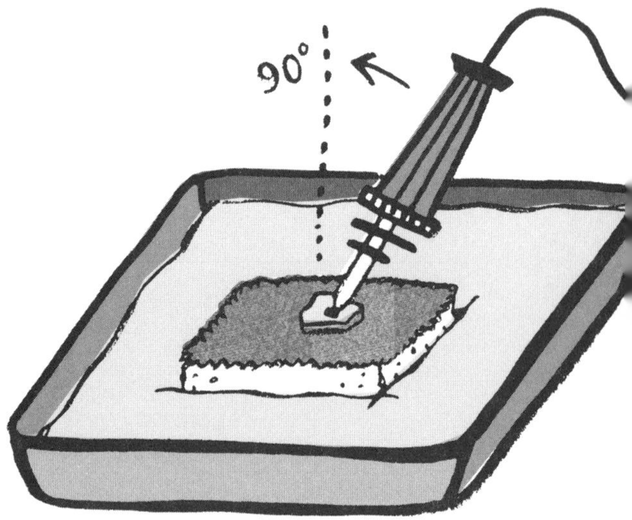

Step 1

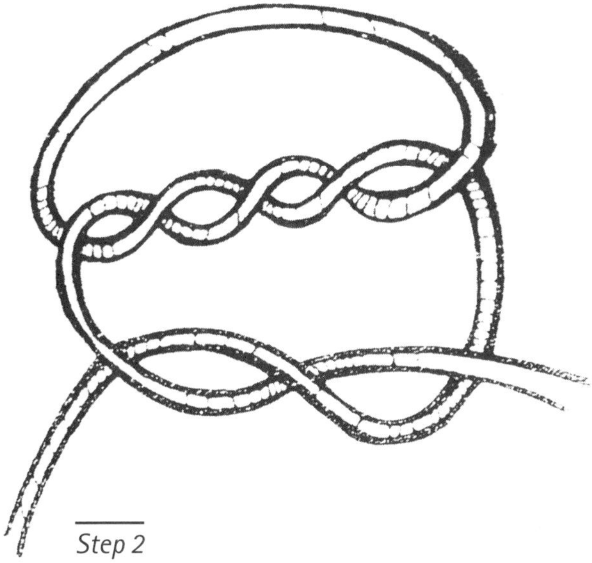

Step 2

Step 2: Cut a 1-foot piece of fishing line for each piece of beach glass you have. Slip one end of the line through the hole in each piece of beach glass and tie the short end off using a surgeon's knot, which is just like a square knot but with an extra twist. Wrap the short end over and around the long end twice, and then wrap the long end over the short end once and pull so the knot is snug against the top of the beach glass. For added security, add a dot of glue to the knot—avoid getting glue on the glass if you can—and let dry. Snip the short end close to the knot. Repeat for all the pieces of beach glass.

Step 3: Sketch out the mobile, taking into consideration the weights of the different pieces of glass. If you have a small scale, you can weigh the pieces to get an idea of how to configure the mobile. If you don't have a scale, you'll have to wing it a bit. But note that if you plan on hanging a piece of driftwood off center of the piece above it, you'll need to compensate with more weight on the other side of the top piece. The entire mobile is like a see-saw, and both ends need to be roughly the same weight. Make sense? To make things easier on yourself, make a rough ladder with your driftwood, drilling a hole in the center of each piece to connect your horizontal pieces of wood in a ladder, or cascading, formation and hang beach glass along both sides of each piece.

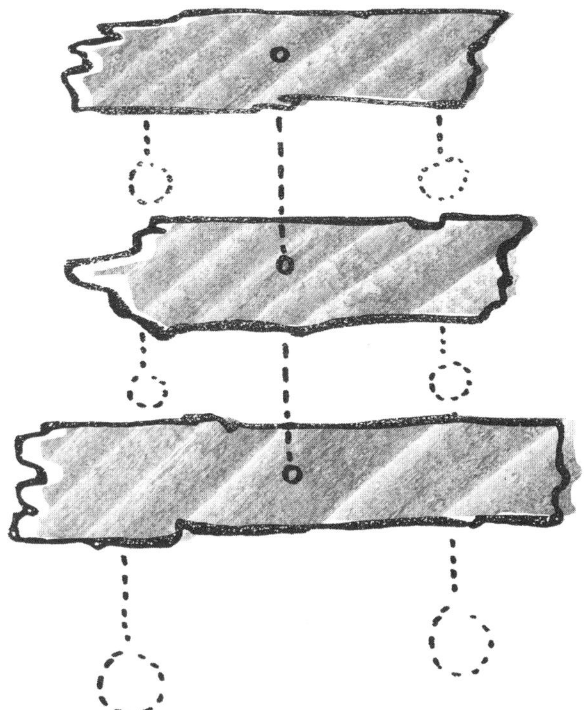

Step 3

Step 4: Now that you've got a general plan for your mobile, take out your driftwood. Mark the spots where you want to drill with a Sharpie marker. Place the wood in a small pan filled with water, so the wood is just covered with water. Using your Dremel tool with the multipurpose drill bit, drill a hole through the wood, using the Sharpie marks as a guide. (If the driftwood is large, you may have to use an electric drill with a longer drill bit.) Start on a slow speed and increase as you drill. After drilling each piece, set it aside to dry.

Step 5: Let's put this beachy bad boy together. Slip a length of heavy fishing line through a hole in the middle of the top driftwood piece and knot it snugly around the wood with a surgeon's knot. Put a dab of glue on top of the knot to secure it. Slip a key ring or large split ring onto the other end of the fishing line and knot and glue it in the same manner. This is the ring that will hang from a ceiling hook.

Step 6: Working from the top down, string each piece of fishing line through a hole in the wood and tie it loosely. Do not glue the knots yet, in case you have to move the beach glass strands to readjust the weight. After each layer has been added to the mobile, hold it up and see if it's balancing well. If it's too light on one side, consider adding another piece of glass or substituting what's there with a heavier piece.

When the entire mobile has been roughly assembled, secure your beach glass strands. Using an awl or a pin, put the point through the middle of each knot and pull the strand free. Now retie the strand using a surgeon's knot and secure it with a dab of glue. Trim off the loose ends.

Note: For a true beach effect, you can also incorporate shells or rocks into your mobile design.

Other Mobile Materials

- hardware, such as washers and bolts
- fishing lures
- medicine bottles
- shells
- bottle caps

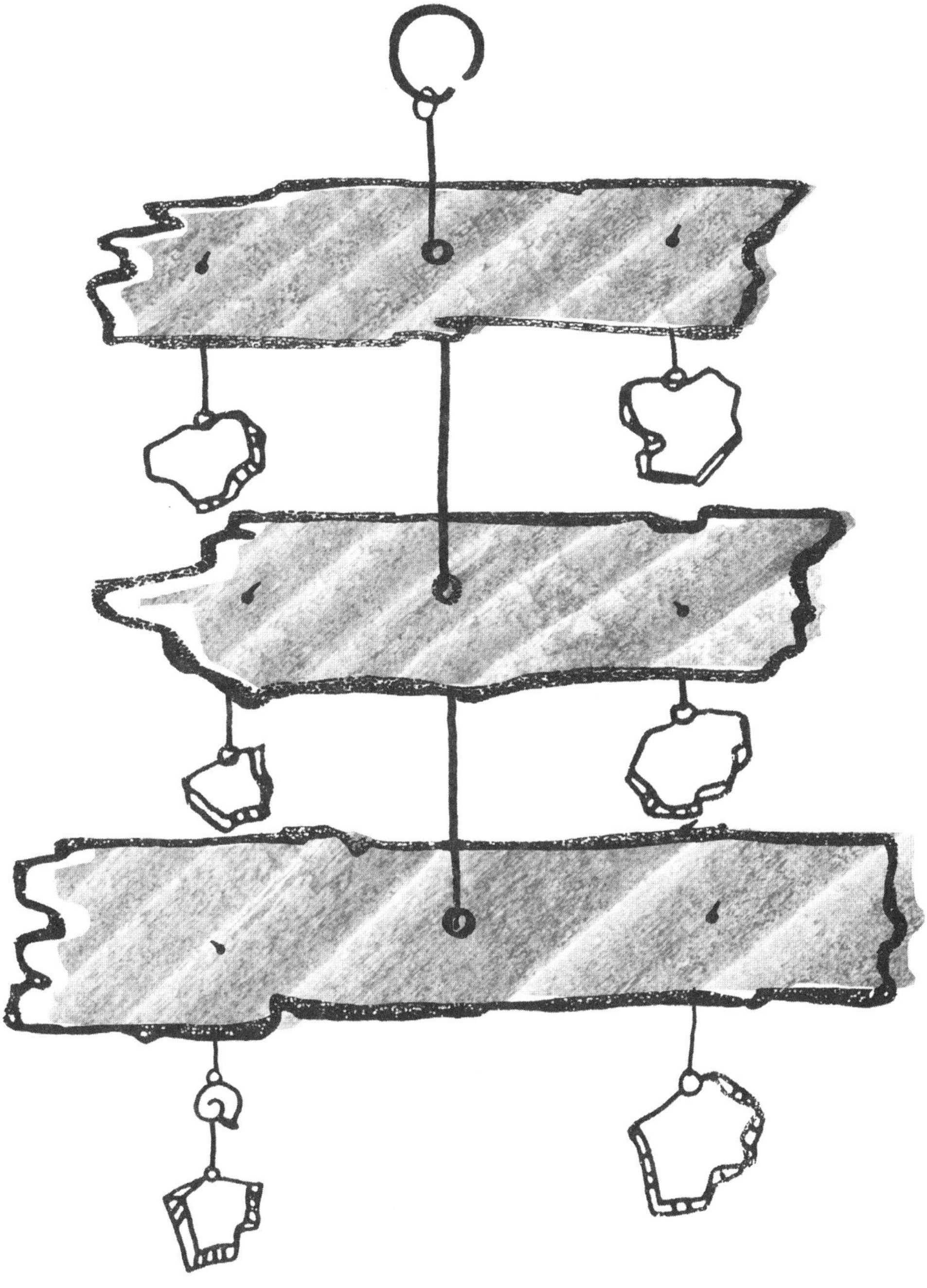

BEACH GLASS CHARM BRACELET

This jewelry project allows you to show off your seaside treasures. I find that making jewelry out of beach glass collected from special trips and holidays makes for a sentimental and distinctive souvenir. And hey, there's always the thrill of the bragging rights. "Yeah, I made it out of stuff I've picked up over the years. No big deal." Be prepared for your friends to start drooling as they stare at your absolutely gorgeous, one-of-a-kind bracelet—a perfect warm-weather accessory for a sunkissed wrist.

You'll need:

- safety glasses
- old kitchen sponge with a rough side
- shallow metal pan
- water
- 20 pieces of small beach glass
- Dremel tool with 1/16-inch diamond drill bit
- cleaning stone for Dremel diamond bit
- 20 7mm sterling silver jump rings
- chain-nose pliers
- 7 1/2 inches of sterling chain with large links
- 2 4mm jump rings
- sterling sliver toggle clasp
- clear nail polish

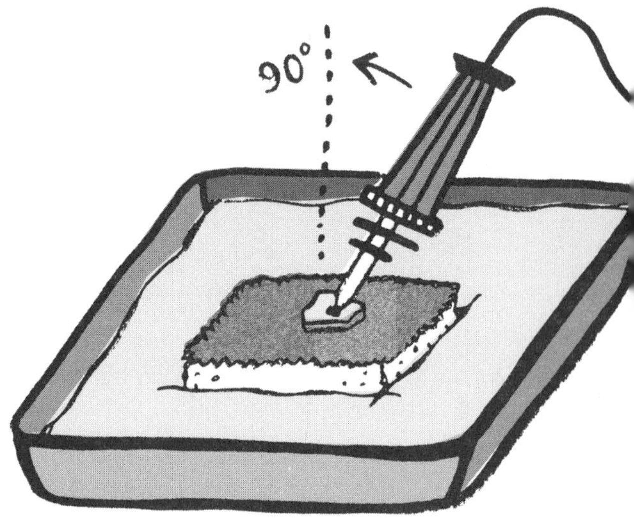

Step 1

Step 1: Don some oh-so-attractive safety glasses. Place a sponge rough-side-up in a shallow pan of water. Place pieces of beach glass on the sponge. To drill holes in the glass pieces, place your Dremel tool with the diamond bit at a 90-degree angle to the glass. It's best to position the hole about 1/8 inch from an edge of the glass so that you'll easily be able to attach a jump ring. Set your Dremel tool on low and don't press too hard; the Dremel will do the work for you. Increase the speed as you get more comfortable with drilling. You'll know when the hole is made as there will be a moment with no resistance. And keep the glass and the area you are drilling damp. You may need to press down on the sponge every so often to keep it wet. Clean the drill bit after every few holes drilled. (Clean the Dremel by setting it to the lowest speed and gently holding the cleaning stone to the edge and tip of your diamond bit, keeping both in the water.)

Step 2: Twist open a jump ring with chain-nose pliers and slip on a piece of beach glass. Pick a link on your length of chain and thread the open jump ring through the link. Close the jump ring. Repeat for the rest of the beach glass beads. You can choose to position the glass randomly on the chain, or for a more uniform look, start with the largest glass piece in the middle and work down in size to each end, counting out your links.

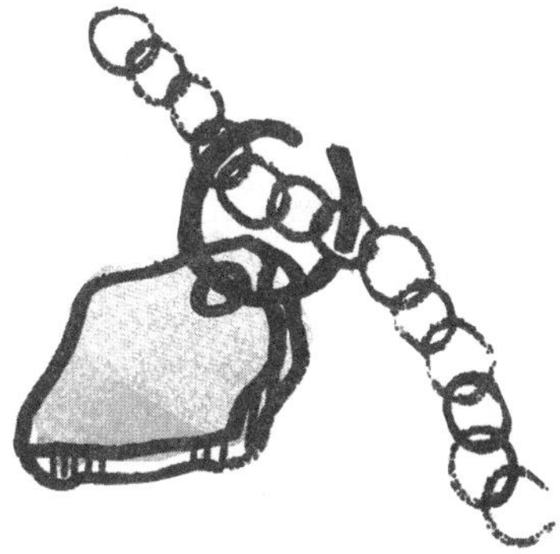

Step 2

Step 3: Twist open a small jump ring and slip it onto the last link of one end of the chain, and then slip on the toggle of your clasp. Close the jump ring. On the other end of the bracelet, twist open the other small jump ring, add the bar component of the clasp, and slip it through the link. Close the jump ring. If you like, you can add a dab of clear nail polish at the join of all your jump rings for added security.

Lickety Split: Beach Glass Sass

If you are lousy with beach glass, add ten to twenty drops of your favorite essential oil to a small bowl of beach glass and set it in the bathroom. You could even put a teaspoon of sand or a small piece of driftwood in the bowl first, add the oil, and then top with the beach glass so the oil evaporates more slowly. If it gets dusty, just rinse with water, allow to dry, and reapply the oil.

ORNAMENT ON THE HALF SHELL

My mom used to whip up these groovy organic Christmas ornaments back in the 70s, made with shells she got from the Holiday Inn restaurant where she worked. She also tole-painted mushrooms on driftwood, découpaged Holly Hobbie-ish heads in frames, and macraméd with a vengeance. I daresay she was a crafty Betty way before her time.

You'll need:

- 8 x 8 inch pan
- water
- old kitchen sponge
- oyster shell, clean
- Dremel tool with multipurpose drill bit
- newspaper
- Rub 'n Buff Finish
- paper towel
- scissors
- image of your choosing (old Christmas and greeting cards work great!)
- Mod Podge Gloss-Lustre sealant
- small foam brush
- 12-inch length of ribbon

Step 1: Fill the 8 x 8 pan with water. Place the oyster shell in the water on top of a sponge. Pick a spot in the top end of the shell where you want to position a hole for the ribbon (think about how you are going to hang your ornament). Make sure that spot is submerged in water. Using a Dremel tool set on low, drill your hole, holding the tool perpendicular to your shell. Don't press too hard, the Dremel will do the work for you. Increase the speed as you get more comfortable with drilling. You'll know when the hole is made as there will be a moment with no resistance. Pull the drill out, turn it off, remove the oyster shell from the water, and dry thoroughly.

Step 2: Spread newspaper on your workspace. With a piece of paper towel, rub a bit of Rub 'n Buff cream over the outside of the shell and on the rim of the inside of the shell to give it a rich metallic sheen.

Step 3: Cut out an image that will fit nicely inside the shell. As this is a perfect Christmas ornament, you may want to pick a holiday

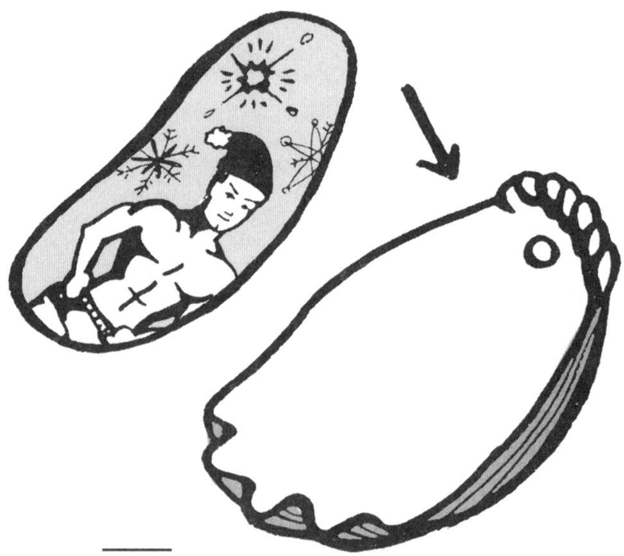

Step 3

image, such as a favorite family photo, snowman, or hunky elf. With a foam brush, coat the back and front of the paper with Mod Podge. Place the image inside the shell and let dry. Now coat the entire inside of the shell with Mod Podge. Let dry and repeat one more time. Let dry.

Step 4: Thread ribbon through the hole and tie it in a knot. Hang your new ornament on your tree and wait for the "oohs" and "ahs."

Lickety Split: Rock Bouquet

Show off your rock collection by placing it in a glass container such as a vase or bowl. You can also place large rocks in a vase and use them as stabilizers when building a flower bouquet. For maximum visual impact, consider color, shape, and size when arranging your rocks. Go all white, for instance, or mix up your rocks for a jubilant display of natural beauty.

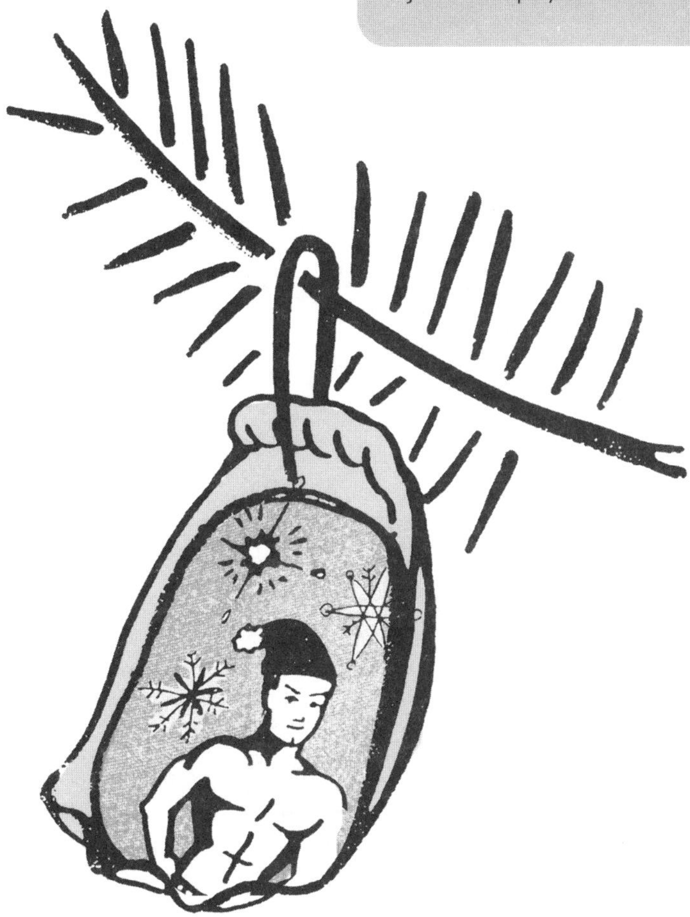

TABLETOP ZEN GARDEN

In this crazy busy world, I have a hard time winding down and relaxing. Forget about yoga or meditation, I don't have that kind of commitment. Instead, I enjoy raking sand in my Zen garden over and over again, creating new designs while I clear my mind. And it's a snap to make your own garden. Just root around in your closet, collect some sand, and pick out a few rocks and shells that have sentimental value or a lovely shape. You'll be blissed out in no time.

Lickety Split: Sandy Toes Foot Scrub

Mix up some clean sand with a bit of olive oil for a makeshift foot and elbow scrub. If you're feeling really indulgent, add a few drops of tea tree oil (a natural anti-fungal and antiseptic oil) or your favorite essential oil to the mix. (See *Working with Essential Oils*, page 18.)

You'll need:

- newspapers
- black matte spray paint
- lid of a sturdy shoe box
- 4 cups sand
- a few of your favorite rocks and shells
- shrimp or salad fork, or toothpick

Step 1: Lay newspapers down in a well-ventilated area (preferably outside) and spray paint one side of the shoe box lid. Let dry, turn over, and spray the other side. Let dry.

Step 2: Pour the sand in your new tray. Place your rocks and shells artfully on the sand. Stack rocks into cairns for a bit of vertical interest.

Step 3: When you need to relax, rake the sand with your fork, and reposition the rocks and shells.

HOURGLASS GAME TIMER

I love a curvy hourglass shape. With my hips and bust, I'm fortunate enough to be able to admire that shape regularly (at least when I'm poured into serious foundation garments). But I don't carry a floor-length mirror around so I thought I'd make another kind of hourglass that I can look at with admiration. With a bit of sand and ingenuity, you too can whip up a cute hourglass that can be used as a game timer.

Step 1

You'll need:

- 2 mini liquor bottles
- 1/3 cup sand
- 1 large 2- or 4-holed button
- serious glue, such as E6000
- stopwatch

Step 1: Empty your liquor bottles. When you've shaken off the hangover, fill one bottle with sand, making sure the rim of the bottle is wiped clean of sand. Place the button over the bottle to make sure that the holes in the button are inside the circumference of the rim (the sand will pass through the button's holes into the other bottle when the hourglass is finished). If your button is set for go, carefully rim the bottle with your glue and place the button, again making sure the holes don't get clogged with glue. Let dry thoroughly.

Step 2: Before gluing the other bottle to the flip side of the button, do a test run. Place the bottle upside down over the button's holes (in basically the position it should be when you finally glue). Get your stopwatch and start it as soon as you flip over the hourglass, holding the two components together. Time how long it takes for the sand to pass out of the first bottle. If you want to shorten the time, pour out a bit of the sand from the second bottle, place the pieces together and retime as the sand passes back into the first bottle. Tweak this until you are happy with the time. (I like to get it as close as possible to 30 or 60 seconds.)

Step 3: With the sand back in the original bottle (the one glued to the button), wipe the button and second bottle clean of sand. Rim the second bottle with glue, turn it over and position it over the button, again taking care to steer clear of the button's holes. Let dry thoroughly. Game on!

Note: If you want to empty more mini liquor bottles (and who doesn't?), make some snappy salt and pepper shakers out of the empties. Simply punch a few holes in the lids (use a nail or small awl) and you're set to spice things up.

EYE MASK

After a long day of staring at a computer or hiking in the bright sun, my eyes are tired. Nothing seems to soothe tired, puffy eyes quite like a nice weighted eye mask, one that just sinks into the eye sockets and smoothes out all cares and creases. I didn't have a good one lying around so I figured I could whip one up. Looking around the house, I soon found everything necessary to make a sturdy, non-leaking mask. (As soothing as an eye mask can be, nothing ruins the effect quite like sand trickling into the eye . . .)

You'll need:

- hourglass-shaped pantyliner
- one 12 x 15½ inch Tyvek bag (FedEx or Priority Mail envelopes work just fine)
- pen
- sharp scissors
- ⅓ yard mid-weight cotton fabric
- cotton or cotton-poly thread
- sewing machine
- measuring cup
- 2 cups of sand, clean and dry
- straight pins
- needle

Step 1: First you'll want to make the liner, the bag that will contain the sand. A pantyliner is the perfect template for your pattern. Stick a pantyliner on the outside of the Tyvek bag. With a pen, trace around the pantyliner. If it's a small pantyliner, trace a line about ½ inch to 1 inch out from the pantyliner. Remove pantyliner. With sharp scissors, cut through both layers so you end up with two pieces.

Step 2: Before sewing the Tyvek liner, fold your fabric in half, with the wrong sides showing (the side that won't show when done), and

Step 1

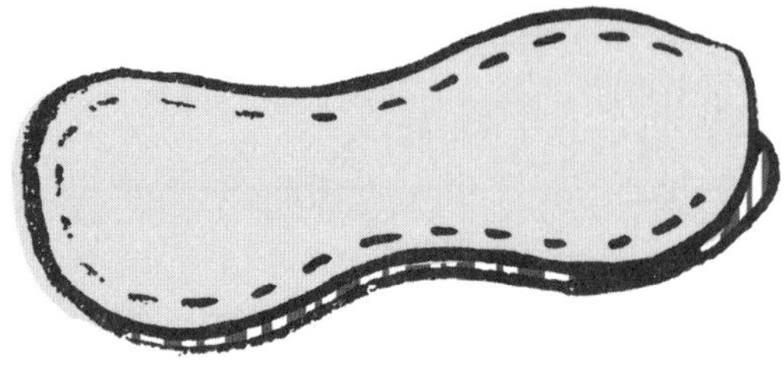

Step 4

trace around your liner, this time 1/4 inch away from the edge. Carefully cut out 2 fabric pieces and set aside.

Step 3: Now it's time to sew the liner. Since this is going to be hidden, don't worry about the raw seams showing. Place the printed sides facing each other—do not pin!—and with a sewing machine, stitch around the perimeter of the two pieces, leaving a 1/8-inch seam allowance (that is, sew close to the edge) and stopping 2 inches from where you started. Do not turn inside out. With a measuring cup, pour the sand into the pillow lining. Do not fill it up, as you want to have a little bit of drape to your pillow. Press the opening together and stitch shut. At the beginning and end of your seam, backstitch a few stitches to secure the closure. Trim the loose ends. Eyeball your pillow; is the seam allowance still a bit wide? If so, trim it down a bit, being careful not to nick the stitches.

Step 4: Now take your two pieces of fabric and pin them together, right sides facing. Sew around the perimeter of the two pieces, starting on a long end, down a short end, and back across a long end, leaving a 1/8-inch seam allowance. Stop before stitching the last short end. Turn pillowcase inside out and place your sand pillow inside. Tuck the open ends under and pin them together. Thread a needle and knot the ends together. Start by pulling your thread through one open end from the inside so the knot is secured and hidden inside your pillow. Using a backstitch (see page 19), hand sew the pillowcase closed and finish by pulling your thread through one piece of fabric and knotting it, hiding the knot inside the pillow.

Step 5: Close your eyes and drape the pillow over them. Rest and reflect on how darn crafty you are.

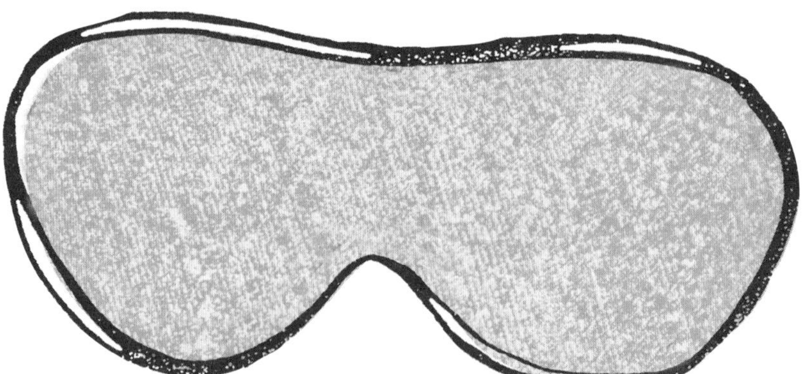

"SANDBLASTED" GLASS VASE

I love the beach—sand, sunscreen, and all—but I don't exactly live near the equator. In fact, the closest I get to tropical is a daiquiri now and then. So I thought I'd bring a bit of the beach to me—literally. I returned from a trip to the Oregon coast with a Ziploc of sand and a burning desire to keep the relaxed beachy vibe going as long as possible. With a bit of glue and a plain glass vase, I whipped up a fun, sandy vase in no time.

Step 1

You'll need:

- clear glass vase
- vinegar and water (in equal portions) in a spray bottle
- masking tape
- newspapers
- small, disposable dish (I used a large pill bottle)
- wooden Popsicle stick or tongue depressor
- 1/2 cup sand, clean and dry
- 1/4 cup Mod Podge Matte-Mat
- small foam brush

Step 4

Step 1: Clean the outside of the vase with vinegar and water. Dry thoroughly.

Step 2: Attach strips of masking tape horizontally around the outside of the vase, starting at the bottom and leaving a 1-inch gap between strips of tape.

Step 3: Lay down newspapers on your workspace. In a small, disposable dish, mix the sand and Mod Podge together with a Popsicle stick or tongue depressor. This makes a sandy paste of sorts.

Step 4: With a small foam brush, apply a thin layer of the sand/Mod Podge mixture to the exposed areas of your vase. When you are done, rinse out your brush and let the vase dry. When the sand mixture has dried, apply a coat of Mod Podge to the sandy stripes. This will smooth out the sandy layer and protect it. Let dry. Remove the tape and enjoy your seashore creation.

NOTES

- You can create vertical stripes by changing the direction of the tape stencil.
- Only wash your vase as needed, and very carefully. Try to wash out only the interior of the vase with liquid, and wipe the exterior with a damp cloth. Too much attention to the exterior could make the sandy stripes erode.

STORMING THE SAND CASTLE

Not all art needs to be permanent. Think about what would have happened if you immortalized your bilevel haircut from the 80s. A masterpiece then, it's most likely a good thing that water and time were able to wash it away. A sandcastle is another transient creation that is fun to create and tweak and fiddle with. If you don't like it, just raze it and start over. I like traditional sand castles for some reason; perhaps I have a lingering princess complex. But I also like to build unexpected shapes in the sand, although I'm still having some problems with that sand stiletto heel.

You'll need:

- beach location with water and sand
- beach bucket
- pen and paper
- spade
- fork, putty knife, butter knife
- bowls, cups, and containers of various sizes
- watering can
- spray bottle
- shells, beach glass, rocks, seaweed, and other found items, optional

Step 1: Pick your location. You don't want your work-in-progress to get washed away but you don't want to be far from the water, either—you'll need it to build your castle. So look at the tide line and the time of day and set up shop accordingly. Gather a bucket of

Step 2

water and maybe even dig a hole in the sand until you hit dampness or even water; you can use this wet sand for your structure.

Step 2: To build a foundation, tamp down waterlogged sand in a 3 x 3 foot square (the footprint of your castle). Gather and mound up wet sand about 3 feet high, trying to keep the cube you are building level across the top. If the middle tends to be higher, no worries. Just keep spritzing and dribbling water over the sand to keep it wet and moldable.

Step 3: Think about what you want your castle to look like; sketching it out can be helpful. Using a putty knife or a dinner knife, start cutting and carving. Cut away areas for doors, windows, and stairs. Use small containers (even an empty pill bottle can work) to pack wet sand in and turn it out on your castle to create towers and turrets. Finish off by using a fork to create water lines around the castle for a moat, or cross hatch markings to indicate brick walls.

Step 4: Decorate your castle if you like. Collect a few found items on the beach. Seaweed can easily double for murky water, a feather can transform into a flag.

Lickety Split: The Sand Storm

Fill jars or glass bowls with clean sand and fill them with candles, dried flower arrangements, brushes and pens, or anything else you want to keep stable and upright.

Step 3

WHITTLE WHILE YOU WORK STARFISH

Some people dig playing with fire or running with scissors. I like cutting up wood with knives. Of course, it needs to be downed wood. I leave the saplings—as delicious looking as they are—alone. I even like going at a piece of driftwood to create something reminiscent of the beach. When I'm in my home in the middle of winter, far away from a tropical paradise, I can look at my cheery whittled starfish and perk right up.

You'll need:

- pencil
- 2 x 4 x 12 inch piece of basswood or another soft wood (such as pine)
- pocketknife or set of wood-carving knives
- newspapers
- 100-grit sandpaper
- foam brush
- ½ pint oil-based primer, like Rust-Oleum®
- ½ pint oil-based paint, like Rust-Oleum®

Step 1: With a pencil, sketch a starfish shape on a piece of wood. You can tweak as you go, so think about a simple one-dimensional shape for now.

Step 2: Whip out your pocketknife or a wood-carving tool (you can buy a set very inexpensively). Lay out newspaper on your workspace. Hold the knife in your dominant hand and grip the wood with the other. With long, shallow strokes, push the blade into the wood, always cutting away from your body. Start by making shallow cuts around your starfish sketch. This will help you get a feel for the knife and wood. Continue to make long, shallow cuts, getting rid of all the wood outside of your starfish shape.

Note: A good way to stay in control of your project, and to show the wood who's boss, is to push the blade into the wood by guiding the knife with the thumb on your non-dominant hand.

Step 3: As you zero in on your starfish, make smaller, more delicate cuts near the pencil lines.

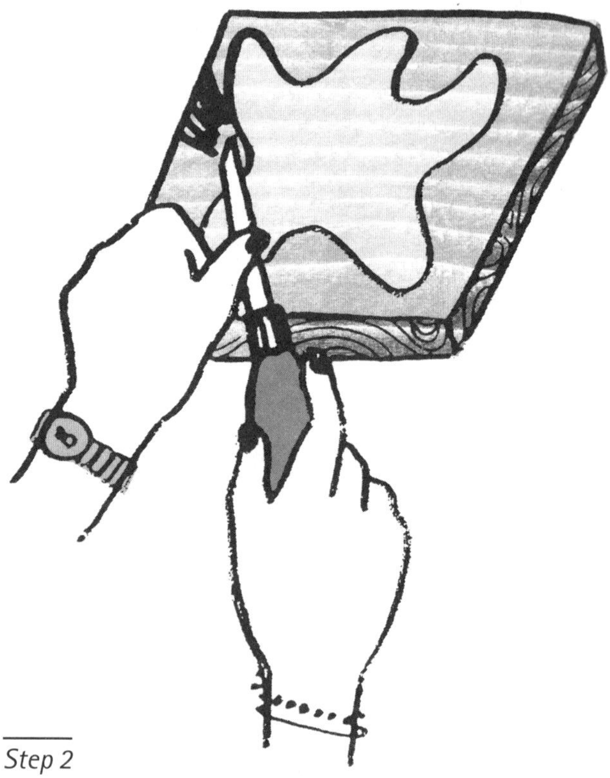

Step 2

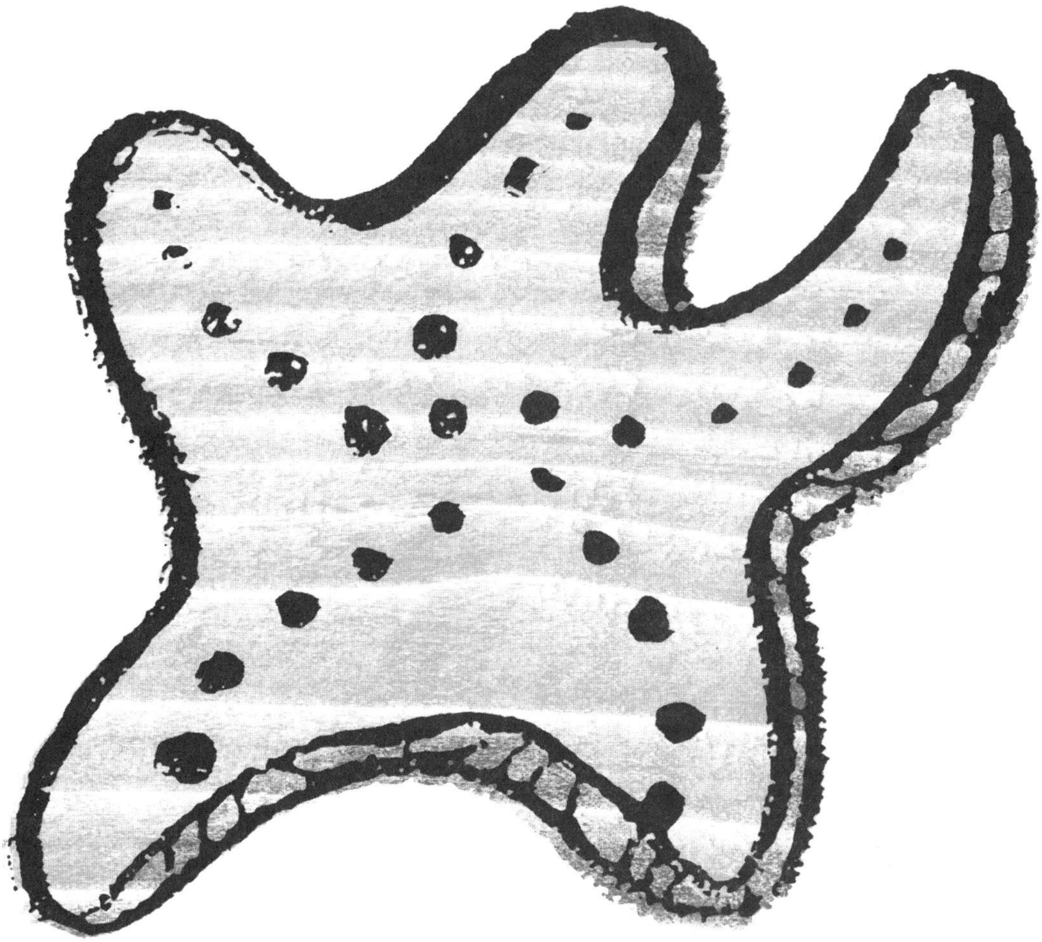

When you have whittled out the flat shape of your starfish, round and refine your creation so it becomes more three-dimensional. Smooth the edges by sanding the wood with 100-grit sandpaper.

Step 4: Lay newspaper down on your workspace. Using a foam brush, paint on a primer and let dry. Now, again with the foam brush, coat your starfish with an oil-based paint. After seeing some unbelievably bright starfish peeking out of tide pools on Orcas Island, I like a poppy orange or purple. Let dry thoroughly.

Place on a bookshelf or, if you're feeling fancy, use an electric drill to make a hole in one of the starfish points and hang it from a ceiling or on a Christmas tree.

Note: For a seriously beachy creation, try to whittle your shape out of driftwood.

SHELL BOWL

I like seeing seashells by the seashore but I also like admiring their graceful form in my home. So in order to enjoy *les fruits de mer* (sort of), I adorned the exterior of a small bowl with shells to create a lovely mosaic and useful vessel. Make three and use them for an ironic take on the shell game.

You'll need:

- newspapers
- mosaic adhesive
- small paintbrush
- small glass or wood bowl
- variety of small shells
- Popsicle stick or spreader tool
- premixed mosaic tile grout
- water
- sponge
- soft cloth

Step 1: Lay newspapers on your work surface. Read the instructions on your adhesive, but some of the easier adhesives work like this: With a small paintbrush, apply a thick coat of adhesive to the outside of the bowl you are going to mosaic. When the adhesive on the bowl's surface becomes a bit tacky (versus runny), brush adhesive onto the rims and insides of your shells. Be liberal with the adhesive; the shells won't lie flush against the surface because of how they curve so you want as much goo gluing the shells to the surface as possible. With the bowl flipped over, cover the exterior of the

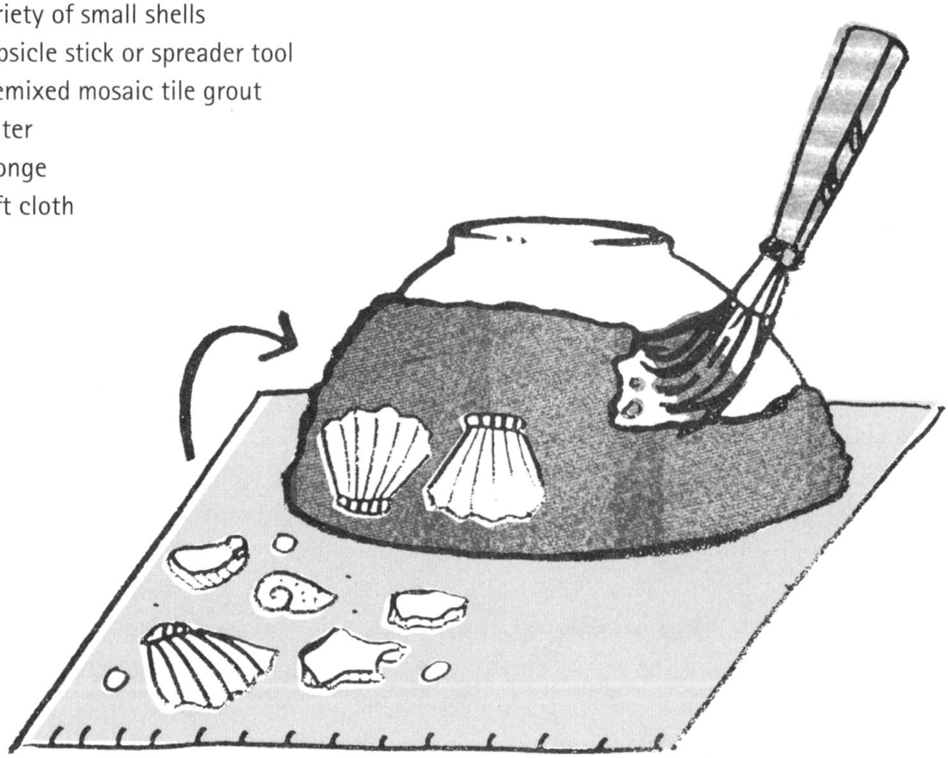

Step 1

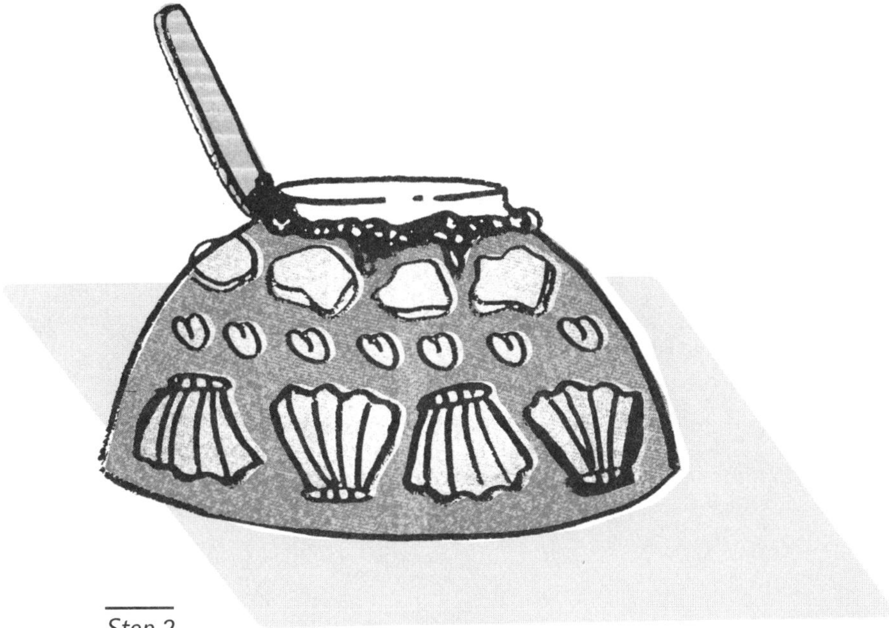

Step 2

bowl with your sticky shells, placing them close together but not touching. Depending on how tacky your base adhesive is, you might have to hold each shell in place for a moment or two until it adheres. Otherwise, you might find the shells slipping off. Let dry, usually twelve to twenty-four hours.

Step 2: Using a spreader tool (such as a Popsicle stick), smear grout into the nooks and crannies around the shells. You won't be able to get the grout level with the shells, obviously, because of their shape but you do want to embed their edges in the grout so they are secure. Let the grout set for a half hour and then wipe the excess off with a damp sponge. When the grout is completely dried, polish the shells with a soft cloth.

NOTES

- Instead of shells, use beach glass in your mosaic.
- When cleaning, try to clean just the inside of the bowl and simply rinse or wipe off the outside shell surface.
- Don't like a certain piece of china or pottery you got as a gift from a taste-challenged relative? Turn it into an interesting and useful bowl or trivet. Simply break up the piece (put it in a towel and lightly hammer it) and use in your mosaic. If anyone asks, just say that you loved it so much that you had to find a way to keep it after it "accidentally" broke.

Chapter 4

IN THE MEADOW

Meadows remind me of picnics and long naps on blankets. I'm from southwestern Michigan farm country and there aren't a lot of majestic mountains in the area to indulge my inner Betty. Instead, I had to take my nature in the form of meadows, cornfields, wild berry bushes, and the occasional marshy area on the side of the road or the railroad tracks. And you know what? I have found a lot of goodies in my wanderings, both then and now. If only I had ever found lavender, I'd have been a blissful Betty. But I've also been geeked to find blackberries, rocks, arrowheads, turkey feathers, and all sorts of weeds and herbs. (I've even been known to find a fella.)

All this talk about meadows is giving me a hankering for picnics and the great outdoors. I think I'm going to organize an alfresco adventure straight away. It'll give me the opportunity to hunt down a pussy willow or two, not to mention some flowers for pressing. And, of course, I get to eat potato salad with gusto. What's not to like about that?

BATH FO'SHIZZLE

For all my posturing about being a Backcountry Betty, I do love me some tub. In fact, I take a bath several times a week in the summer and nearly every night in the colder months. That is, every night that I'm not out camping or exploring the wilderness, obviously.

And I like to have a ball in the bath. To that end, I like to whip up fizzy bath balls and watch the bubbles explode all around me, releasing essential oils to suit my mood. Bath fizzies are a snap. Seriously, when I found out how easy they were to whip up, I sort of became outraged at how much various companies charge for these tub treats. I had to take a deep breath and inhale some chamomile to calm down. In fact, I made a chamomile bath ball out of all the dried chamomile I've been collecting.

For six to eight bath balls, you'll need:

- scissors
- 1 pair pantyhose
- 1 cup dried chamomile
- parchment paper
- 1 cup citric acid
- 2 cups baking soda
- large mixing bowl
- approximately 20 drops chamomile essential oil (you can also add a few drops of another complementary oil, such as peppermint or ylang ylang to the mixture). (See *Working with Essential Oils*, page 18.)
- 1/4 cup witch hazel in a spray bottle

Step 1: You may have seen some of those gorgeous bath bombs, the ones with dried rose petals or other herbs poking out of the ball, in fancy shops. Well, the problem with these is that the dried flotsam and jetsam leave a mess behind in the tub. When you have to clean the tub after you climb out, it sort of defeats the relaxing properties of the bath now, doesn't it? To eliminate that problem, enclose the herbs for your fizzy treats in four-to-five-inch circles cut from an old pair of nylons (cheesecloth or muslin works just as well). Place a small mound of chamomile in the center of a circle and knot it tightly at the top. Make six to eight of these balls and set aside.

Step 2: Lay a sheet of parchment paper on the counter. Combine the citric acid and baking soda in a large mixing bowl, using a whisk or fork to mix thoroughly. Sprinkle the essential oil into the mixture and mix again, making sure to evenly distribute the essential oil through the powder. Doesn't it smell divine?

Step 3: Spray the witch hazel into the mixture with one hand. With the other hand, continue to mix the contents of the bowl. You'll feel the powder starting to get damp after several minutes. When you can clump the mixture in your fist, it's time to form the balls. Work quickly as the witch hazel is already evaporating. Take one of your hosiery balls in your

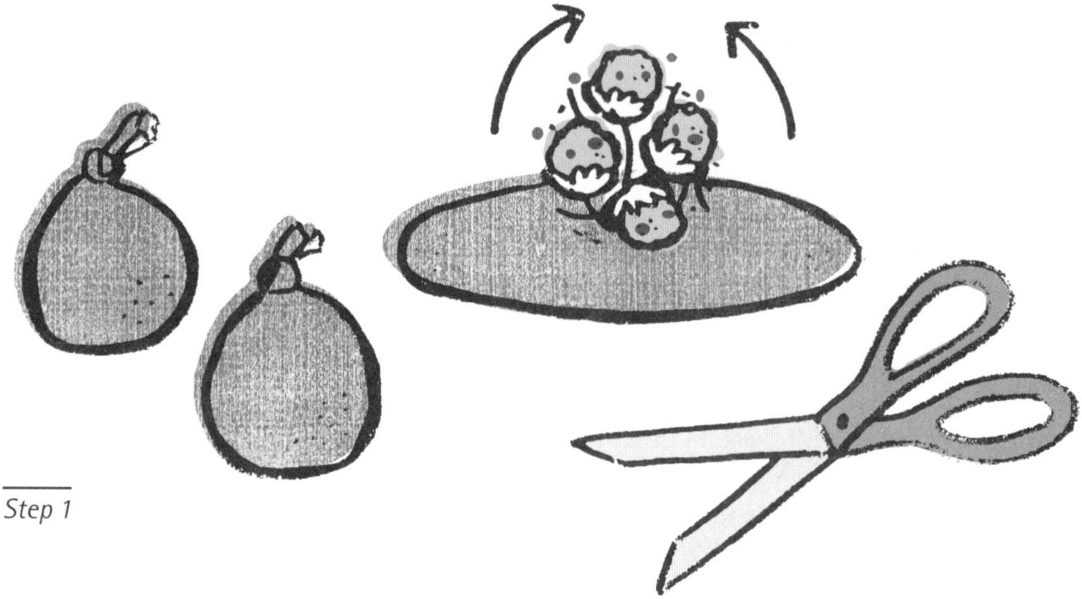

Step 1

palm and quickly coat it with the fizzy mixture, packing it tightly into a small snowball of sorts. Place it on the parchment paper and move onto the next one. Let your bath fizzies dry (keep them away from water until ready to use!). You can either store them in a plastic container, seal them in baggies, or wrap each one in acetate to give as gifts. Wash your hands thoroughly when you are done.

Step 4: When you are ready to rock your tub, draw a bath and as you sink into the water, drop your bath ball in. Enjoy the fizzy fragrance.

Note: You can also make bath fizzies by loading your mix (without the chamomile ball) in a plastic ice cube tray. Wait a few minutes for the mix to dry and harden, and then gently pop out your bath fizzies.

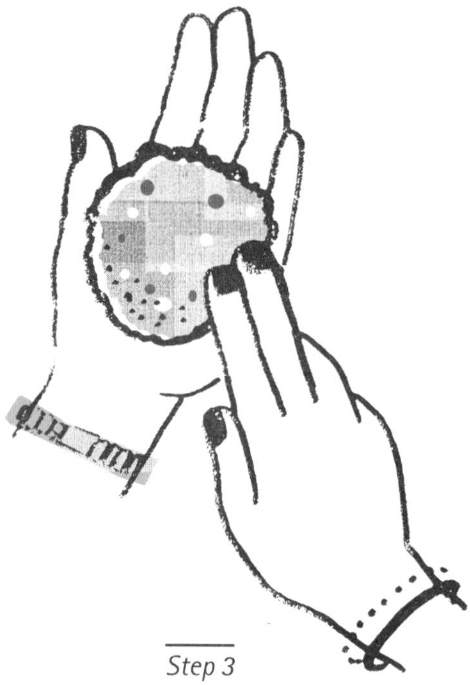

Step 3

MOSS BALLS

When it's time to decorate for the holidays, why not forgo the crazy light displays and the animatronic Santa, and opt instead for a more rustic and completely cool display of mossy balls? They are an unexpected way to showcase the colors of the season!

You'll need:

- scissors
- red yarn
- tapestry needle
- 6 Styrofoam balls
- newspaper
- sheets of moss, clean and dry
- hot glue gun
- Dremel tool with #561 multipurpose bit (looks like a drill bit)
- long piece of driftwood or branch
- fishing line
- 2 screw-in utility hooks

Step 1: Cut six 15-inch lengths of red yarn. Thread a tapestry needle with one piece of yarn. Push the needle at a shallow angle into a Styrofoam ball so that the needle pokes through. Pull the needle and yarn through the ball and tie the yarn in a square knot (right over left, left over right) leaving a long tail. (The yarn will eventually be affixed to your driftwood rod.) Repeat with the other five balls.

Step 2: Spread newspaper on your workspace (moss is messy). Gather your moss and separate it into small clumps.

Step 3: With a hot glue gun, thoroughly coat an area of your Styrofoam ball with glue

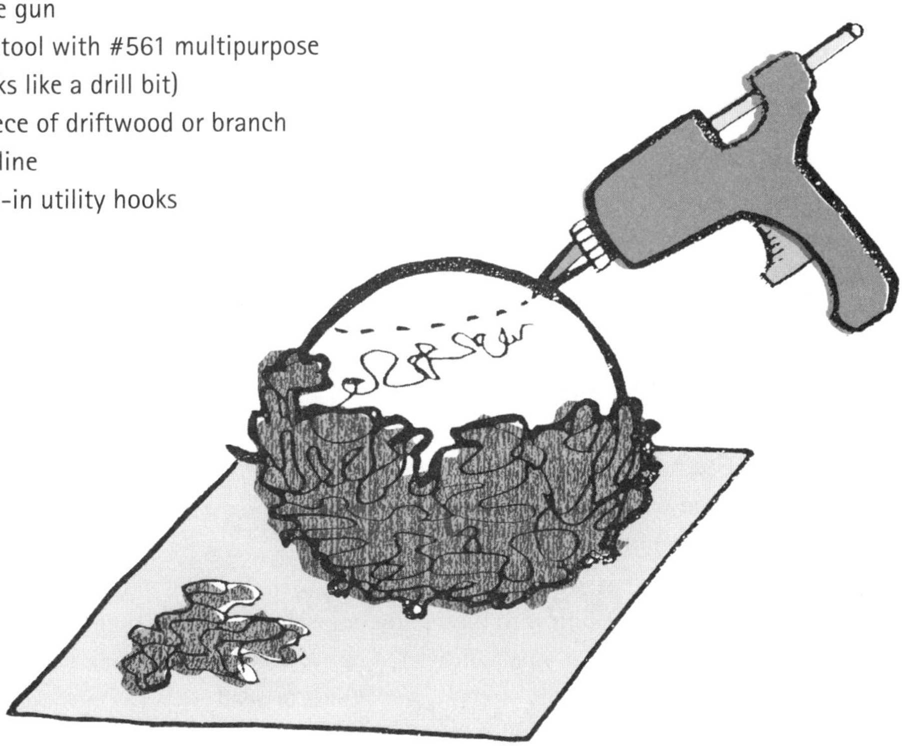

Step 3

and quickly press the moss onto the glue. Work your way in this manner around the ball until it is completely covered with moss. Set aside and let dry. Repeat on the rest of your balls.

Step 4: With your Dremel tool, drill a hole completely through your driftwood (if your wood is thicker than 1 inch, you'll need to use an electric drill instead). Repeat at seven regular intervals along your wood. You should have eight evenly spaced holes when you are done.

Step 5: Thread the yarn tail of one ball through one of the center holes and tie to the driftwood. Put a dab of glue on the knot and let dry. Clip off the excess yarn. Working from the center of the driftwood rod to the ends, tie on the rest of your balls. Do not use the outside holes. You can tie the balls at the same level or you can mix it up and hang them at varying lengths.

Step 6: Now it's time to hang this sucker. Tie a length of fishing line to each outer hole on your driftwood. Use a surgeon's knot, which is just like a square knot but with an extra twist. Wrap the short end over and around the long end twice, and then wrap the long end over the short end once and pull so the knot is snug against the top of the wood. For added security, add a dot of glue to the knot and let dry. Create a loop on the end of each piece of fishing line and secure it with a surgeon's knot. Measure the length between your two outside holes and screw two hooks into the ceiling with the same distance between hooks. Hang your gorgeous, festive moss balls!

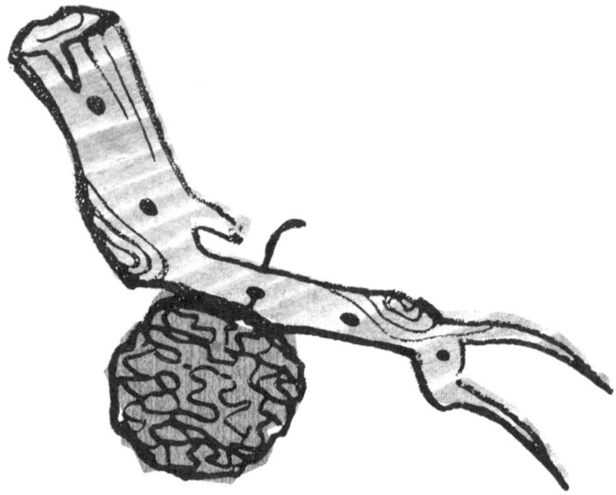

Step 5

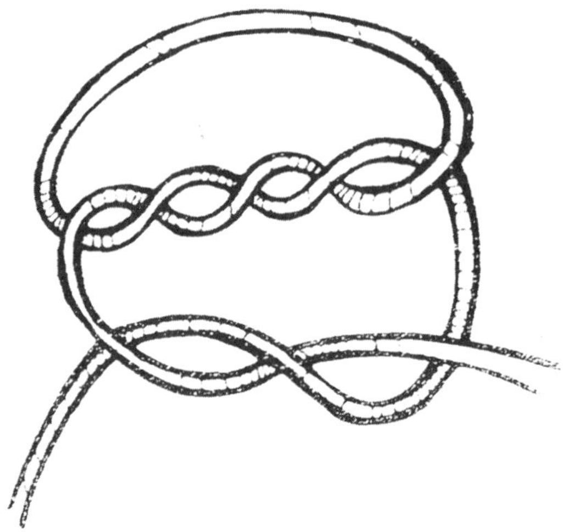

Step 6

Note: If you don't have space for the driftwood rod or birch branch, you can hang your moss balls on your tree or display them in a bowl instead.

Lickety Split: Dry Herbs

Gather a bundle of herbs, tie them by the stems, and hang them upside down in a dark, dry place. When they are dry, you can use them in potpourri, dried flower arrangements, or even lotions and potions (such as a lavender bath tea or feverfew tea).

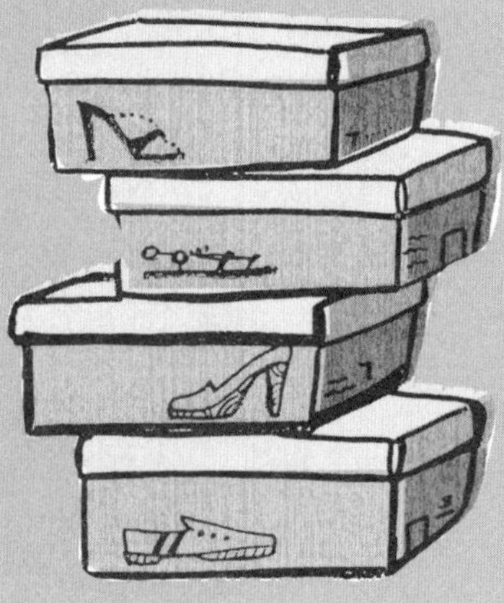

THE CASE OF THE DRAWER LINER

I don't know about you, but I like my drawers (both kinds, if you get my drift) scented. I personally fancy lavender. Whenever I walk by a lavender bush, I can't help but rub a bud between my fingers and sniff my hand all the way down the block. It looks weird but I don't care. I'm too blissed out. So I try to bring some of that euphoria to my lingerie drawer by laying a lavender liner under all the frilly knickers and bras. It's both indulgent and ingenious and you can personalize it with stamps and fabric paint or even a bit of embroidery or iron-on transfers if you're so inclined. These are easy gifts for those people who claim to have everything. I bet they don't have a hand-made lavender drawer liner. I'm just saying . . .

You'll need:

- iron
- old pillowcase
- starch
- heavy cardboard
- foam brush
- fabric paint
- rubber stamps
- tailor's chalk
- 2 cups dried lavender buds
- sewing machine
- thread (cotton or cotton-poly blend)

Step 1: Wash and press the pillowcase with starch so it's stiff. Slip a piece of heavy cardboard inside the pillowcase.

Step 2: Using a foam brush, apply fabric paint to rubber stamps of your choosing and stamp the pillowcase. Reapply and repeat as desired (you can use one dominant stamp, a row of stamps, or random stamping all over the pillowcase). Let dry thoroughly (usually twenty-four hours). Remove the cardboard.

Step 3: Using tailor's chalk, mark a 1-inch seam at the open end of your pillowcase. Now measure the width of the pillowcase, not counting the 1-inch seam, and divide by four. For instance, a standard pillowcase is 26 inches wide so subtract one to get twenty-five and divide by four to get 6¼ inches.

Using the tailor's chalk, mark off three vertical lines every 6¼ inches. Add ½ cup of dried lavender to the pillowcase, making sure it is all in the bottom fourth of the pillowcase. Sew a seam, following that first vertical line at 6¼ inches, to secure the lavender in the pillowcase. Now add another ½ cup of lavender and sew another seam at the middle mark. Add another ½ cup of lavender and sew the third seam. Add the last of the lavender and sew your final seam.

Step 2

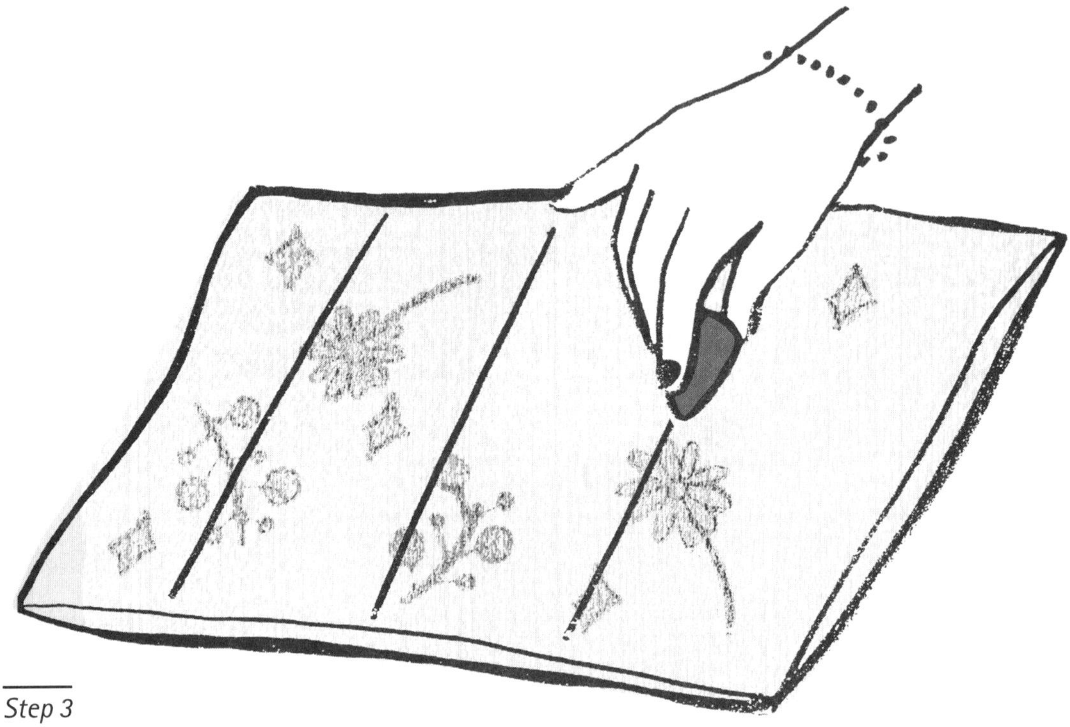

Step 3

Step 4: Line your lingerie drawer with your fragrant liner, making sure to spread the lavender evenly.

Note: If you don't have the perfect stamp, make one out of a potato. Cut a large russet in half and blot the cut surface with a paper towel. With a Sharpie marker, draw a shape (abstract and large is a good way to go) and then cut around the design so that the shape is raised about 1/4 inch. When you've created a stamp, test it out on a sheet of paper and then apply a thick coat of fabric paint and go to town on your pillowcase.

Lickety Split: Set the Table

Use found items to whip up a fancy table setting: vines can tie napkins, small shells can serve as salt cellars, large leaves become coasters or placemats, pinecones can easily hold place cards. Let your imagination run wild with your wilderness finds!

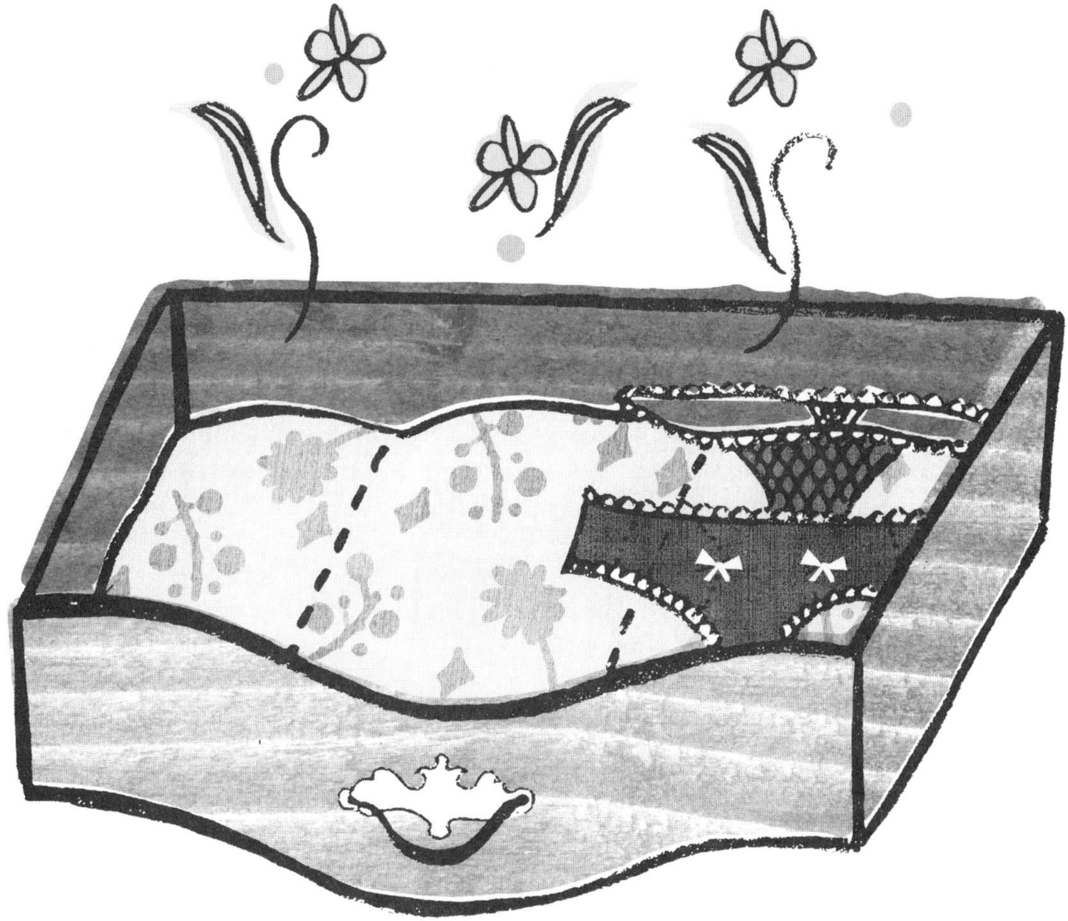

TO DYE FOR

I love all berries, except, sometimes, blueberries (don't ask). I love everything about them: the shape, the smell, the way they explode in your mouth, the seeds you find stuck in your teeth long after the berry is gone. Living in the Pacific Northwest, I'm able to enjoy marionberries, loganberries, and even a salmonberry now and again. I thought I'd extend my love of all things berry to my wardrobe, pulling out a vintage slip that, while gorgeous, I figured could use a bit of brightening up. So I reluctantly decided to forgo stuffing my pie hole with all the berries I collected on my walk around the lake and instead used them to create a berry good dye for my unmentionables. (You can also substitute beets or red cabbage if you can't get your hands on some berries.)

You'll need:

- rubber gloves
- 4 pints ripe berries (blackberries will dye your slip purple, while raspberries will give you a rosy pink hue)
- 9 1/3 cups water and 4 gallons water
- 3 large stainless steel pots
- cheesecloth
- 5 1/2 ounces alum
- white silk or cotton slip, or another small light-colored garment or piece of fabric
- large wooden spoon

Step 1: Put on the rubber gloves and some old clothes you don't mind staining (an apron might be in order here). Keep those gloves on throughout the entire dying process. Clean the berries and add them to the 9 1/3 cups of water in a large pot. Bring to a boil and then let simmer for one hour. Strain the mixture into another large pot using cheesecloth to catch all the fruit. Continue to simmer the dye bath.

Step 1

Step 2: Dissolve the alum (which you can usually find at the grocery store in the spice aisle) in 4 gallons of lukewarm water in another pot. The alum will make sure your new color doesn't fade.

Step 3: Wet the slip separately and then drop it into the alum water and give it a stir. Let the water come to a boil and cook your slip for twenty minutes.

Step 4: With the wooden spoon, remove the slip, wring it out, and then add it to your dye bath. Check that the color is evenly distributed. Remove when you've achieved the desired color, keeping in mind that the color will be lighter once it dries. If you want a really rich color, take the pot off the burner and let the garment soak in the dye bath overnight. Rinse in cold water and let air dry.

Note: Always hand wash your dyed creation separately in cold water.

Lickety Split: Pussy Willow Bouquet

A few twigs of pussy willows in a jug or vase make every room cool, no matter the design style.

FLAVORED HONEY

I think I was a bear in another life because I love honey so, so much. I think I'd even brave a hive of angry bees for fresh honeycomb. It's pretty easy to infuse alcohol with fruit or herbs so I thought I'd try it with honey. The results? There are no words. And if there were, I wouldn't be able to speak anyway. My mouth would be full of honey.

You'll need:

- 2 Mason jars
- large kettle
- water
- tongs
- 2 cups organic raw honey
- small saucepan
- 3 tablespoons dried herb, such as lavender or fireweed
- cheesecloth

Step 1: Sterilize a Mason jar in a hot water bath: place the jar and lid in a large kettle of boiling water for ten minutes, remove with tongs, set on a clean towel and let dry thoroughly.

Step 2: Warm up the honey in a small saucepan over low heat. Place your herbs in the Mason jar. Pour the honey over the herbs and seal the jar loosely. Allow the herbs to infuse the honey for two weeks, and then strain the honey through cheesecloth and transfer to another sterilized Mason jar. This gorgeous honey is lovely in tea or on toast . . . or both! Or consider wowing other Betties by presenting them with a small jar of their own.

Note: Make sure you are using an ingestible herb for your infusion.

FIRE POWER

Call me crazy, but I like creating things out of cast-off items, stuff people don't look at twice. It makes me feel like a crafty, female MacGyver. Humble straw is one such often–overlooked item. Back in the day, folks slept on straw mattresses. Animals still sleep on it. But sweet-smelling straw is also handy fire fodder, especially if it's twisted and braided into a nifty kindling stick. It may seem simple, but I'll tell you what: it's a perfect gift for those annoying people who have everything. Everything, that is, except straw kindling sticks.

You'll need:

- large rubber band
- 1 bushel of straw (12-inch pieces, or longer if possible)
- cotton or wool yarn or cord (optional)

Step 1: Rubber-band twelve strands of straw together 1 inch from one end. Divide the strands into three groups of four: hold two sections in one hand, dividing them with your index finger, and hold the other section in your right hand.

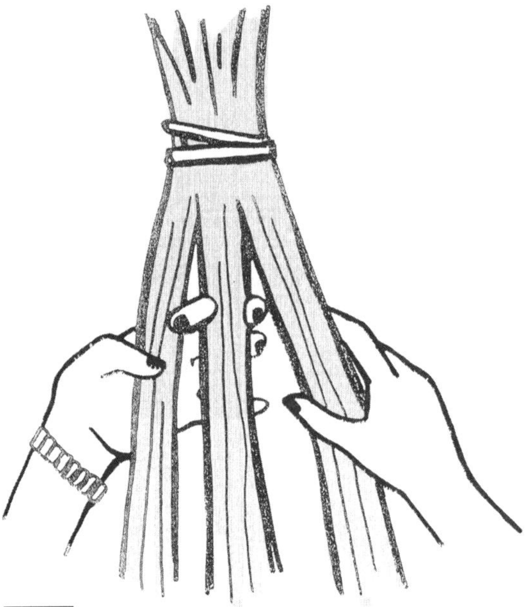

Step 1

Step 2: Let's braid! Lay the right section of straw over the center section and then the left-most section over the new center section. Continue alternating the right and left sections over the center section until you come to the ends of the straw pieces. Each straw stick should be about 12 to 15 inches long so if the original sections don't reach that far, weave in four new strands to take over for each section. It's okay if the ends stick out. These should look a bit, uh, rustic. When you reach the end, tie off your stick with a piece of straw (you could also use colored cotton or wool yarn or cord to snazzy it up, if you like). Remove the rubber band and tie off the original end with straw as well.

Step 3: Create a whole pile of these kindling sticks and set them in a basket by the fire for when you need to start or stoke a fire.

Note: These make unusual but much appreciated gifts for anyone with a fireplace or wood stove.

Lickety Split: Wreaths of a Feather

For an unconventional door ornament, push a variety of feathers into a Styrofoam wreath.

HOTPOURRI

Potpourri doesn't have to be a smelly bunch of buds and petals found on your aunt's toilet tank. Turn potpourri into the hottest, hippest way to scent a room with this fragrant mix that smells like the deep woods.

You'll need:

- assortment of pressed flowers (see page 89 for basic flower drying techniques)
- pine essential oil (See *Working with Essential Oils*, page 18.)
- juniper berries
- pine needles (use the needles that fall off the tree after Christmas)
- small pinecones
- cedar wood chips
- large bowl or jar

Step 1: Press an assortment of flowers, and dry some juniper berries and pine needles. (See page 89 for basic flower-pressing techniques and page 74 for herb-drying instructions.) I'm not including quantities here because potpourri can be inexact, free, and joyous. Like making stew, just add in what you have on hand and doctor it up.

Step 2: When your materials are ready, simply mix petals, berries, pine needles, a few pinecones, and a handful of cedar chips in a large bowl or jar. Sprinkle pine and/or juniper essential oil onto the mix and place near a window so the fresh scent of the outdoors can waft through your home.

Note: To prolong the scent, cover your potpourri when not in use. To freshen up your Hotpourri, add a few drops of essential oil.

Chapter 5

IN YOUR OWN BACKYARD

You don't have to travel into the wilderness to find some great items for naturally crafty projects. Just head to one of your favorite places: the backyard. If you don't have any outdoor space, forage in your friends' and family's backyards, preferably with some tasty vittles on the grill and a cocktail in hand. I'm sure they'll let you hunt and gather. Just ask nicely and send them a leaf-stamped thank-you note.

Our urban wilderness is a treasure trove of materials for craftacular projects. From a flower bed to a berry bush to a simple leaf off the tree in the front yard, your options are boundless—without having to trek to the forest, desert, or seashore. Just breathe in the fresh air and take the time to look around you as you walk out the door, even when you have an action-packed day ahead of you. Not only will you give yourself a serious dose of oxygen, you just might find an empty birds' nest or perfect four-leaf clover. You never know when it will be your lucky day.

THE LEAF MOTIF TEE

I love a good leaf motif and I'm always looking for ways to adorn my clothing, housewares, and furniture with leaf shapes. I'm currently obsessed with the shape of ferns and the elegant ginkgo leaf, and I have a lifelong affinity for maple leaves (maybe I'm a closet Canadian). Anyway, it's a snap to adorn a lowly t-shirt or tank top with a leaf or another favorite nature shape.

You'll need:

- iron
- t-shirt
- heavy piece of cardboard
- straight pins
- newspaper
- foam brush
- leaves or other found items (see sidebar this page for ideas)
- fabric paint
- parchment paper
- small rolling pin or brayer

Found Flora Stamp Fodder

Flat items work best. For instance:

- feather
- fern frond
- holly leaf
- lily pad
- maple seedpod (can be used as angels' wings or turkey feathers)
- money plant (also known as honesty)
- seaweed
- a vine
- wheat stalk

Step 1: Wash and press a t-shirt. Slip a heavy piece of cardboard inside the shirt, smoothing but not stretching the area to be stamped. Pin the shirt to the cardboard. Set aside on a flat surface that's covered with newspaper.

Step 2: Working on a flat surface covered in newspaper, use a foam brush to coat the underside

Step 2

of your leaf with a thick layer of fabric paint.

Step 3: Carefully position the leaf, paint side down, on the t-shirt. Place parchment paper over the leaf. With pressure, roll over the leaf and parchment paper with your rolling pin. Resist the urge to do this more than once or twice, as the leaf may shift and distort your paint job.

Step 4: Remove the parchment paper and leaf. Leave the cardboard in place and allow the shirt to dry (it takes twenty-four hours to dry and three days to be ready for washing). Wash and wear with pride.

NOTES

- Rubber stamps can also work nicely in lieu of natural items.
- You can use this same technique—swapping out fabric paint for acrylic paint—to make handmade cards and gift tags that are sure to impress.

Step 3

PRESSED FLOWER POWER

Honestly, I find a lot of pressed flowers to be sort of fussy. I think it's because they seem precious and non-functional, like all the ceramic lady head planters my grandmother had littered around her farmhouse. But with some restraint, I've learned to create some lovely and useful items with a few of my favorite wildflowers. Below are some tips on pressing flowers using just a few materials. Give it a whirl. You will quickly learn to love the art of pressed flowers and you just might start adorning everything you can get your hands on.

You'll need:

- backyard flowers for pressing
- sharp scissors
- Ziploc bag
- telephone books
- newspapers
- Post-it Notes

Step 1: Collect your flowers. Heading out in the afternoon with sharp scissors, cut the flower from the stem (some Betties like pressing the stem as well for various projects so cut with your end project in mind), making sure that the flower is dry before snipping. Drop them in a Ziploc bag and press them within one or two hours of cutting, again making sure they are dry. (Gather flowers in the afternoon so that any dew has evaporated.)

Step 2: In lieu of a flower press, gather some telephone books (as many as possible) and newspapers. Fold a newspaper in half vertically and then in half horizontally.

Step 2

If you like the idea of including the stem with your flower, the stems that work best are the ones that are more delicate and thin (like the flower head itself). A thicker stem may create an air pocket that will prevent a flower from drying properly. You can press the intact flower head, or deconstruct the flower and use individual petals. For the latter, separate the petals, place them on one side of the folded newspaper. Arrange them in the order that you pulled them off in case you want to replicate the original flower shape in a design. Make sure no petals are touching. Fold over the newsprint so the petals are covered, place them in the middle of a telephone book, and then cover with several more telephone books or other heavy flat objects (cinder blocks are especially good if you happen to have a few lying around). Use a Post-it Note to label what's in each newspaper batch. You can just tag the newspaper that is sticking out or you can write on the newspaper directly.

Step 3: Inspect your flowers after a week. If the flowers or petals are still limp, transfer them to new newspaper and replace them in the telephone book for additional drying time. Make sure they are perfectly dry before using them. See page 91 for a groovy project for your pressed flowers, but you can also embellish all sorts of things—postcards, bookmarks, even wrapping paper—with some Mod Podge, paper, and pressed flowers.

Note: Store pressed flowers in the original press (i.e. the telephone book) so they stay as flat and dry as possible.

Step 2

Pressable Flowers

A few of my favorite flora to press include:

- apple blossoms
- baby's breath
- black-eyed Susan
- cherry blossoms
- chrysanthemums
- daisies
- dogwood blossoms
- ferns
- hydrangeas
- leaves
- money plants (really called "honesty" but I like saying "money plant" better)
- pansies
- poppies
- Queen Anne's lace
- roses

Avoid plants that have high water content, such as irises.

PRESSED FLOWER KALEIDOSCOPE

With just a few colorful pressed petals, create a work of art that looks like a playful kaleidoscope. True, it doesn't turn or change but you can create more than one. A series of these framed beauties looks just incredible adorning a wall. And it's a wonderful way to create a souvenir of a favorite place or vacation. Press flowers from a beloved locale (like your backyard!) and enjoy the memories and visual beauty year-round. Or think about creating one for each new adventure you experience, be it in the wilderness or in the neighborhood.

You'll need:

- 8½ x 11 inch sheet of white paper
- compass
- tweezers
- assortment of pressed flowers (see page 89)
- pencil
- ruler
- 2 pieces of 8½ x 11 inch cardstock
- sharp scissors
- small paintbrush (I prefer bristle to foam)
- Mod Podge Matte-Mat
- double-stick tape
- 8 x 10 inch frame

Step 1: On a white piece of paper, plan out your kaleidoscope design. Using a compass, create a 4 x 4 inch circle. Using tweezers, place a small petal or flower close to the center point of your circle. Directly opposite the petal, place another petal of similar size and shape (you are basically mirroring the first petal). Work around the center point in this manner, placing two identical petals opposite each other. Now create a second ring in the same way, mixing up colors as you go. You want a riot of hues complementing and contrasting with each other.

Step 2: After tracing out a piece of cardstock that's 5 x 7 inches and another that's 8 x 10 inches, cut out the cardstock with a pair of sharp scissors. The larger size will serve as your mat and the smaller size will back your kaleidoscope so pick colors accordingly. For this project, I like a white background, so my mat is black or even a bright color.

Step 3: Starting from the outermost rings and working toward the center, brush the back of your petals with Mod Podge and carefully place them on your 5 x 7 cardstock. (Tweezers can again come in handy when handling the delicate petals.) Mod Podge one ring of petals

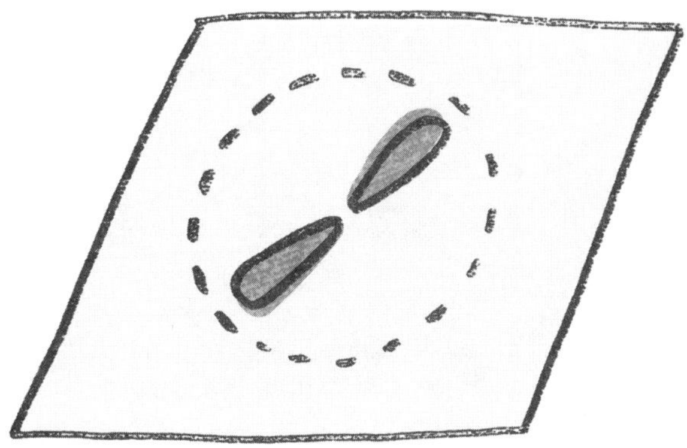

Step 1

at a time, slightly overlapping each new inner ring until you reach the center. Let dry and then, with your paintbrush, apply a thin layer of Mod Podge to the top of your design, and let dry.

Step 4: On the back of your kaleidoscope art, apply a piece of double-stick tape to each corner. Position it in the middle of the 8 x 10 cardstock. Open up the back of your frame and place your creation in the frame. Close the back and admire your gorgeous floral kaleidoscope.

Step 3

Lickety Split: Rochambeau Paperweight

Grab a favorite rock and paint a sheet of paper on one side and scissors on the other. What a cute way to secure your papers or stop your door. Get it? Rock, paper, scissors?

Lickety Split: Nifty Nosegay

Create a simple nosegay by gathering smaller flowers (such as Sweet William or violets), cutting the stems to the same length, and wrapping a rubber band and ribbon around the stems.

Lickety Split: Bird in the Home

Find an empty birds' nest? Bring it in and turn it into a rustic way to display different-colored pebbles that look like eggs. Look for small oval-shaped stones, preferably speckled.

JUNGLE BOOGIE LAMPSHADE

I hate overhead lighting so my home is tricked out with all sorts of lamps with low lighting. Better for attracting the wily male, sexy lighting also makes Betties glow. It's like candlelight without the fear of fire. To bring a little jungle fever into my home I've whipped up several one-of-a-kind lampshades that will make any Betty or wild manimal feel as if they are in their natural habitat. This is my favorite.

You'll need:

- variety of pressed ferns
- square lampshade frame
- newspapers
- matte black spray paint
- ruler
- 8½ x 11 inch piece of cardstock or cardboard
- pen
- cutting mat
- X-Acto knife
- 4 8½ x 11 inch laminating pouches
- laminating machine (your local copy shop usually has one)
- paper hole punch
- 24 1-inch loose-leaf rings
- 25-watt light bulb

Step 1: Press your ferns. See page 89 for a flower-pressing primer.

Step 2: While your ferns are being pressed, prep your lampshade frame (www.lampshop.com has some very simple ones that work beautifully). Spread newspapers outside and spray paint your frame. Let dry and add a second coat. Let dry thoroughly.

Step 3: Measure each side of your lampshade frame and subtract ¼ inch from each side. These will be the dimensions for the four lampshade panels. With a pen and ruler, create a template for each side with a piece of cardstock or cardboard. Using a cutting mat, cut out your template with an X-Acto knife.

Step 3

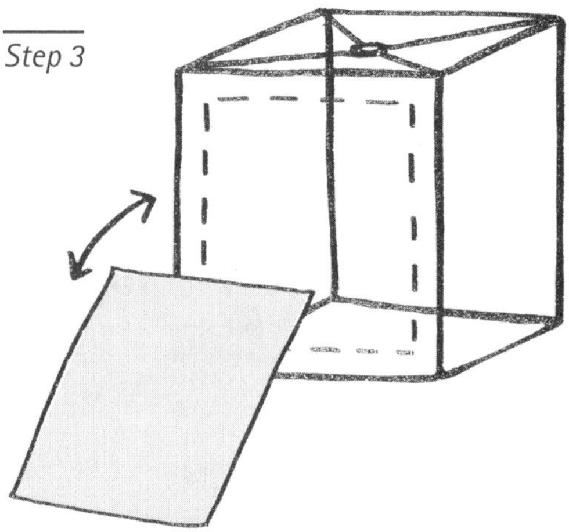

Step 4

Step 6

Step 4: When your fern leaves are pressed and prepped, place them in a laminating pouch. I like to position one large leaf vertically but you could go crazy with loads of smaller leaves and cover the entire sheet. Send each sheet through a laminating machine (follow your machine's directions!) and allow to cool.

Step 5: When all four panels have been laminated to your satisfaction, it's time to cut them to the right specs. Place one laminated sheet on a cutting mat and position your template over it. With a ruler and X-Acto knife, cut out the panel, following the lines of the cardboard template. Repeat for the other three panels.

Step 6: Measure each panel along the top edge and divide by three. This is where you'll want to space out the holes for the two top rings. For instance, if the top edge is 9 inches long, you'll want two holes at 3-inch intervals. Make sense? Just bear with me. Using your ruler and punching ¼ inch from the edge, punch a hole at the two intervals. Do this only on the top edge of each panel.

Step 7: Measure each panel vertically (they should all be the same height) and divide by five. This is where you'll want to space out your holes for the rings. If the height is 15 inches, for example, you'll want four holes at 3-inch intervals. Using your ruler and punching ¼ inch from the edge, punch a hole at the four intervals. Do this on both vertical sides of your panel.

Step 8: It all comes together here. Open up your loose-leaf rings and attach each panel to the top of the frame. Now thread the ring through a hole on the vertical edge of a panel, slip it around the frame, through the hole in the adjoining panel, and close. Each vertical ring will be securing two adjoining panels to the frame. Cool? Okay, connect the rest of the panels to the frame and you're done. Screw in a 25-watt bulb and enjoy the great outdoors without stepping outside.

Step 8

STRAWBERRY FIELDS FOREVER MASQUE

I know your instinct is to shove all those wild strawberries you found on the side of the house or next to the lake into your gullet. I'm with you. I love me some fresh berries and not just in my mouth. Barring any allergies or skin sensitivities, strawberries are a terrific way to tone your skin. Those mighty fruit acids are great for oily skin. And the raw honey has all sorts of crazy healing and soothing benefits for your skin. I met a beekeeper last year and she talked for a good twenty minutes about the miracle that is raw, unprocessed honey.

You'll need:

- 5 wild strawberries
- small bowl
- fork
- 1 tablespoon raw, unprocessed honey
- 1 tablespoon finely ground oats

Step 1: Mash the strawberries in a small bowl with a fork until they are pulpy but not runny. Drizzle in the honey, add the oats, and mix well.

Step 2: Using your fingertips, spread your facial masque onto a clean face in long sweeping motions. Let sit for ten minutes and rinse off. Follow up with your favorite moisturizer.

Note: Patch test this masque on your arm. Place some masque on a Band-Aid and affix to your inner arm. If, after several hours, you aren't experiencing any irritation, you are probably good to go. Be aware that skin sensitivities can crop up later on.

If there is no reaction other than smooth, refined skin, proceed with applying to your face and relaxing.

Chapter 6

IN THE URBAN JUNGLE

Even if you can't get out on the trail with regularity (which is a shame, really, since you have such cute fleecy jackets and snappy hiking boots), there are loads of materials that you can pick up and use from your urban or suburban environs. Just look in the recycling bin if you don't believe me. I know; the idea isn't exactly appealing, but with a bit of ingenuity you can make a great candle holder out of an aluminum can or a lush bouquet out of shredded magazines. Seriously. Just apply the leave-no-trace ethic to your trash, and recycle common items into functional and funky objects.

TICKET-STUB KEYCHAIN

This is a rad project for a favorite ticket stub (Bon Jovi's *Slippery When Wet* tour, for instance, or maybe that's just me) or other paper memento that has sentimental value.

You may remember baking Shrinky Dinks in the oven when you were a wee Betty (you know, a couple of years ago). Well, you can now buy shrink plastic paper that goes through an ink-jet printer. Ingenious, I know.

You'll need:

- scanner
- computer
- Photoshop or other photo software
- ticket stub from a favorite concert, sporting event, ski lift, etc.
- ink-jet printer
- shrink art plastic sheet, suitable for an ink-jet printer
- scissors or X-Acto knife
- paper hole punch
- toaster oven or oven
- 2 small squares heavy cardboard
- parchment paper
- 2 binder clips
- potholder
- newspaper
- Mod Podge Matte-Mat sealant
- small foam brush
- chain-nose pliers
- key ring

Step 1: Scan your favorite ticket and open up the jpg file in Photoshop (or the photo software that comes with your printer or computer). Resize the image to approximately two to three times the size of what you want the final piece to be. Shrinky Dinks shrink to one-half to one-third of their original size, and other brands shrink slightly differently, so you'll have to experiment.

Be sure to read the instructions on the shrink art paper you purchased. In general, you'll want to lighten the image either in your photo software or in the printer settings (when the paper shrinks, it darkens the image). Load your printer with a sheet or two of shrink art paper. Select the paper type (if your printer doesn't give you the specific option, just choose "Other Specialty Paper"). Print out your ticket image.

Cut out the ticket with sharp scissors, slightly rounding the corners. With a paper hole punch, punch a hole near the edge of one short end so you can affix the key ring later.

Step 2: Preheat your toaster oven or oven to 325°F.

Step 3: Place your ticket on a piece of sturdy cardboard that is covered by parchment paper. When the paper heats up, it will curl, sometimes onto itself. To prevent the paper from sticking to itself while curling, I like to place a piece of parchment paper on top of the shrink art item as well, securing the parchment paper loosely with binder clips. Place the cardboard in the oven and keep an eye on it. The shrink art plastic sheet will curl (or try to) and then flatten back out while it's shrinking. When it has stopped wasting away, using tongs or a potholder, remove the cardboard and place another piece of cardboard over your ticket and press down to ensure a flat piece. Let cool for 30 seconds or so. With a potholder, carefully remove the still-hot binder clips and release the ticket. Looks pretty cool, right?

Step 4: The ink-jet ink doesn't completely adhere to the shrink plastic so you'll have to coat it with a sealant. (Otherwise, if the plastic gets wet, the color will spot and run.) I like Mod Podge but there are other sealants and resins on the market that will work as well. Lay down some newspaper and with a small foam brush, apply a thin layer of sealant to the printed side of the shrink art plastic and let dry. Flip over and apply sealant to the back side, and let dry.

Step 5: With chain-nose pliers, pry open the key ring and feed it through the hole of your ticket. This ticket may not get you in to see your favorite band any more, but as a keychain, it will open a few doors!

Note: If you'd rather make a luggage tag, cut a thin rectangular slit in your cut-out item before baking instead of punching a hole in one end. After it has baked and cooled, slip an old pet collar through the long hole and buckle it. You're done. For your luggage tag info, consider using a business card as your image.

Step 3

Step 4

GYM
BON JOVI

UN CENTAVO AFORTUNATO JEWELRY

I don't know about you, but I pretty much pick up every coin I spy on the ground. I've even darted out into traffic to rescue a coin or two. I figure the lucky pennies I gather will protect me from being clocked by someone driving while talking on a cell phone. It seems to have worked out okay so far.

When I travel, I also embrace change. I love seeing all the different designs, shapes, and sizes that other countries come up with. Of course, with the Euro, my delight has been dampened, but no matter. This is a great project for those foreign coins that you weren't able to unload in duty-free before your plane took off. If a coin already has a hole in it, even better.

It's illegal to deface U.S. currency but I'm pleading ignorance on other countries' policies. Please be advised that I'm not advocating making a lucky *penny* necklace or anything. Seriously.

NECKLACE

I like keeping my lucky coins and souvenir coins close to me, so I whipped up a pendant and earrings featuring my good-luck charms. Be prepared for "oohs" and "ahs."

You'll need:

- 1 foreign coin
- 2-hole metal punch
- chain-nose pliers
- sterling or silver-toned base metal jump ring (preferably oval)
- clear nail polish
- 16-inch silver ball chain and connector clasp

Step 1: Insert your coin into the larger of the two hole punches. Align your coin so you are drilling a hole in the top of the coin. Slowly twist the bit until you feel the coin give, which means the hole has been made. Unscrew the bit slowly until the coin drops

Step 1

off. If you try to pull the coin off, you could break the bit.

Step 2: With your chain-nose pliers, gently twist open the jump ring (do not pull the two ends apart to open or you risk weakening or breaking the ring). Slip the coin on the ring and twist the ring until the ends are snugly joined. For further protection, seal the join of the jump ring with a dab of clear nail polish. Let dry.

Step 2

Step 3: Slip your coin pendant onto the ball chain (you know, the kind of chain that's used for dog tags), put it around your neck, and secure with the little clamshell-like closure that is used with ball chain. You're done. Luck be a lady tonight!

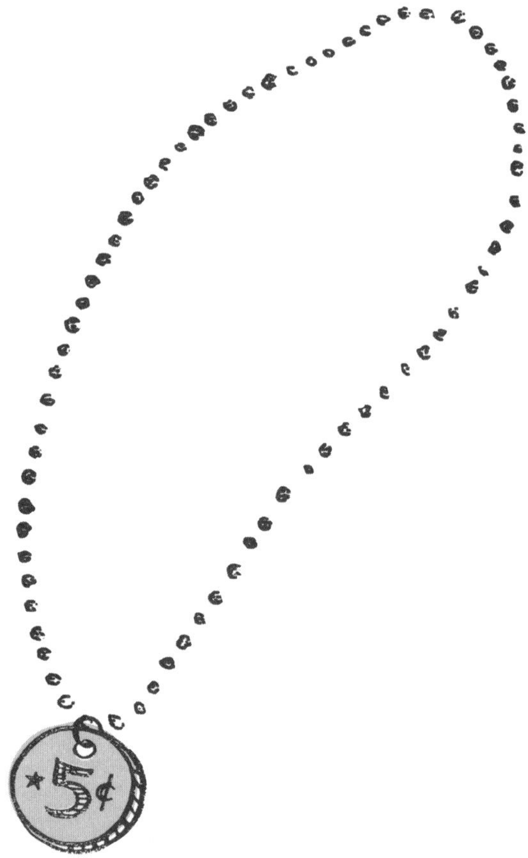

Lickety Split: Jewel Case Frame

Make a picture frame—complete with stand—with a CD jewel case. Simply remove all of the liner notes and packaging and carefully disconnect the two pieces of the case. Now turn the top piece around and reattach to the bottom piece, fitting the pegs into the holes. With the top piece flipped, the bottom of the CD case acts as a base that will sit on a surface and prop up the front side. Using double-stick tape or small foam dots, affix a favorite snapshot or Polaroid photo to the front of the jewel case. Voila! Music to your eyes.

EARRINGS

If you'd rather make some dangly earrings, you'll need to drill four coins. I think it's fun to have a bit of variety on each ear so consider making one earring with the front facing on the top coin, and the back facing on the bottom coin. For the other ear, switch the order (i.e. the back side on top and the front side on the bottom).

You'll need:

- 4 foreign coins
- 2-hole metal punch
- chain-nose pliers
- 6 sterling or silver-toned base metal jump rings (preferably oval)
- 2 sterling or silver-toned base metal ear wires
- clear nail polish

Step 1: Insert your coin into the larger of the two hole punches. Align your coin so you are drilling a hole in the top front of the coin. Slowly twist the bit until you feel the coin give, which means the hole has been made. Unscrew the bit slowly until the coin drops off. If you try to pull the coin off, you could break the bit. Repeat on the opposite end of the coin, so you wind up with a hole at the top and bottom of the coin.

Step 2: The second coin will form the lower half of this earring. With the back of the second coin facing up in the hole punch, align the coin so the hole is at the top of the image. Slowly twist the bit and make a hole in the same manner as in step 1. You don't need a second hole in this coin so let's move on.

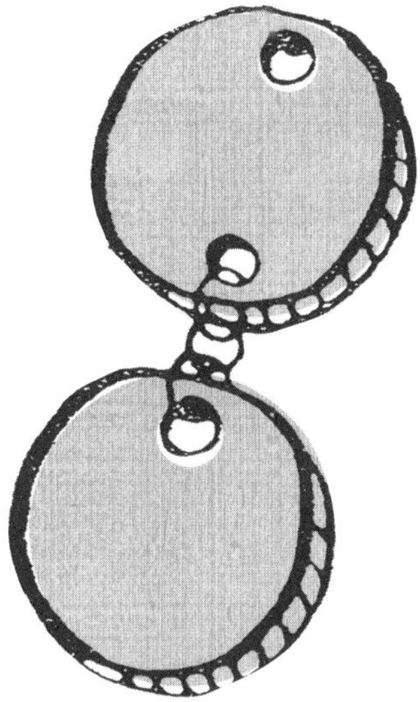

Step 3

Step 3: With your chain-nose pliers, gently twist open a jump ring. Slip the one-holed coin on the ring and twist the ring until the ends are snugly joined. Now, add a jump ring to the bottom hole of the two-holed coin. With the front facing out on the top coin and the back facing out on the bottom coin, join the two by slipping a jump ring through the jump ring on each coin. Make sense?

Step 4: To finish the earring, using your chain-nose pliers, twist open the loop on an ear wire, slip the earring on via the top hole of the top coin, and close the ear wire.

Step 5: Repeat for other earring, this time reversing the order of the coins (the back side gets two holes and goes on top; the front gets one hole and will dangle at the bottom).

Snazzy, don't you think? Think of all the attention you'll enjoy while wearing these beauties.

LAUNDRY BASKET BALL

Transform your ex-boyfriend's wool sweater (or an unfortunate gift from someone who just doesn't get your taste or size) and create an ingenious felted dryer ball. Forget about those dryer sheets; a felted ball of yarn works surprisingly well when it comes to keeping the snap and crackle out of your garments.

You'll need:

- 100-percent non-machine-washable wool sweater
- crochet hook
- knee-high hose
- cotton string
- clothes washer
- clothes dryer

Step 1: The first thing you have to do is say goodbye to a wool sweater as you know it. If you have an ex-boyfriend's sweater lying around, now is the time to make it into something useful. Cut the ribbing off at the waist and look for a loose thread. Unravel some yarn and wrap it tightly around your finger to get it started and then continue to roll it into a ball, about 3 inches in diameter. Cut off the yarn and, with a crochet hook, pull the loose end deep into the middle of the ball.

Step 1

Step 2: Place your ball into the toe of a nylon knee-high and tie it securely with a piece of cotton string. (You can felt several balls at a time in one knee-high.) Throw the knee-high into the washer with a load of dirty laundry and set the water temperature to hot. Toss the ball in the dryer with your laundry as well. When the cycle is complete, snip the string off the knee-high and remove your dense, felted ball. If it's not felted to your satisfaction, repeat the wash and dry cycle.

Step 3: Add another thick layer of wool around your ball, again tucking in the end with a crochet hook. Wash and dry it again in the same manner as step 2. After the dry cycle, remove your felted ball.

Step 4: To prevent static cling, throw the ball in the dryer with wet clothes.

Note: For fresh-smelling laundry, sprinkle a drop or two of an essential oil (like rosemary or eucalyptus) on your ball before adding it to the dryer.

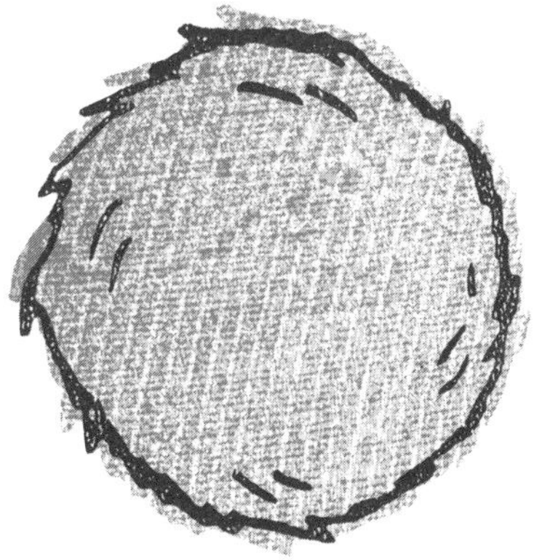

Lickety Split: Bra Strap Headband

Create a cool headband for the trail with an adjustable bra strap. Simply snip a strap off of an old bra and sew it together to create a loop. The adjustable nature of the bra slide will allow you to customize the strap to your head. Black always works, but you can also use wacky-colored bra straps or dye one to suit your needs.

BETWEEN THE SHEETS LAUNDRY BAG

You'll be Queen for a (Laundry) Day when you whip up this simple yet stylin' laundry bag. This project is perfect for the beginning Betty seamstress. The shape is large and forgiving—you can practice sewing straight seams without fear of failure. And once you've made this handy bag, consider sizing it down proportionately and using different fabrics. You'll find these bags have loads of uses.

You'll need:

- iron
- two 20½ x 32½ inch pieces of fabric, cut from an old cotton sheet (if you have a brightly patterned sheet, so much the better)
- straight pins
- thread (polyester or a cotton-poly blend)
- sewing machine
- safety pin
- two 50-inch lengths of nylon cord (I found mine at the hardware store)

Step 1: Press fabric. With right sides facing, pin together with a few straight pins—a straight pin every inch or so.

Step 2: Using a ¼-inch seam allowance and starting 2¼ inches from the top edge, sew down along a long side (reinforce the beginning and end of your seam by backstitching), across the shorter side, and up the other long side, ending 2¼ inches from the unsewn top edge. You have just sewn the sides and bottom of your bag, and left the top raw in order to create a tube for the drawstrings.

Step 3: Keeping your bag inside out (with right sides still facing), press a ¼-inch fold along the top edge. Now fold the top edge over 1 inch and pin down on both sides (be careful to pin just two layers of fabric; don't pin through all the fabric). Sew across each side, leaving a ⅛-inch seam allowance (you want to sew through and secure the ¼-inch fold on each side of the bag). Do not sew shut the 1-inch vertical opening on each end; we'll need those in a minute. Now that you've sewn both top edges down, check out all your seams. If necessary, tack down the ends with a few stitches to reinforce where the vertical side seams and horizontal top seams meet.

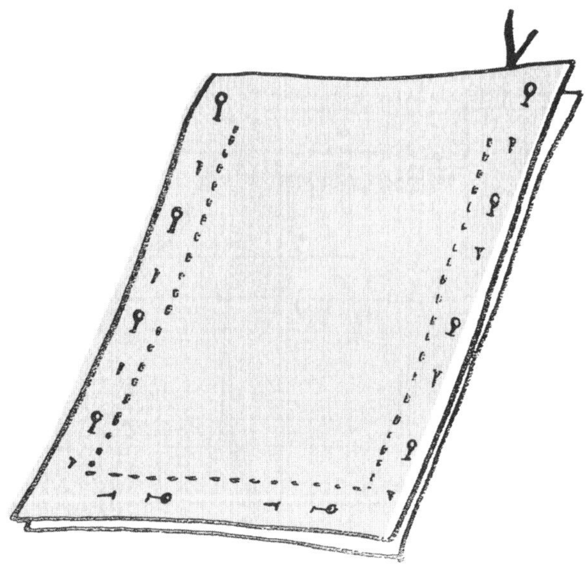

Step 2

Step 4: You and your bag are almost done. Turn it right side out. You're feeling pretty proud of yourself, aren't you? Well, you should. Poke a safety pin through one of the 50-inch lengths of cord. Now, using your safety pin as a lead, feed the cord through the canal on one side, and then back through the opposite side. Remove the safety pin and knot the two ends of the cord together. Starting from the other end, string another piece of cord through the sides in the same manner, knotting the two ends together on the other side of the bag. Yep, that's it! This also makes a great bag to tuck away on a camping trip or a long vacation because you can separate your less-than-savory garments from your clean clothes.

Step 4

ALUMINARIA

As a Betty, I absolutely adore turning trash into treasure, at least something pretty and useful. To that end, I have been experimenting with aluminum cans, as I rack up a lot of them in any given week. My cat, Mac Daddy, enjoys wet food that comes in tiny gold cans, while I make sauces and soups that require me to pop open a can with regularity. So, I have made quite a few "aluminaria," tea light holders out of aluminum cans. And after some trial and error, I've even managed to fool a few people into thinking that I actually bought the can candle holders. They are *that* transformed. Make a few in different sizes and different patterns and you'll have a Betty-ful way to light a party.

You'll need:

- large aluminum can
- water
- 4 cups of brown rice, rock salt, or sand
- large leaf or feather
- parchment paper
- Sharpie marker
- towel
- packing tape or duct tape
- large nail
- hammer
- newspaper
- small can of acrylic spray paint, in color of your choosing
- small can of spray sealant
- tea light

Step 1: First things first: eat whatever is in the aluminum can. I used a large can of peeled tomatoes (for a kick-ass pizza sauce, in case you were wondering), but I also whipped up an aluminarium from a small can of cat food.

Thoroughly wash and dry the can. Stabilize the can for hammering by filling it with a mixture of water and brown rice (it doesn't absorb water as fast as white rice), rock salt, or sand. Freeze the can for several hours.

Step 2: Trace your favorite leaf or feather, or draw a freeform image (stars, flowers, a stiletto heel, whatever you fancy) on parchment paper with a Sharpie. Go over it again to make sure you have a strong, graphic line for your design. Take the can out of the freezer and wipe as much condensation off of the outside of the can as possible. Tape the parchment paper to the outside of the can, taking care to position the image where you want it. I like to tape the

Step 2

paper to itself so it makes a sort of cozy around the can; if the can is damp from the freezing process, the tape won't stick.

Step 3: Place your nail on the tracing at a right angle to the can. Firmly hit the nail with the hammer, making sure to puncture the can. Following the tracing, make holes at regular intervals until you've completed your design. Remove the parchment paper. Turn the can over in a bowl until the rice/water mixture melts. Clean out the can and let it dry.

Step 4: Lay newspapers down and in a well-ventilated space (preferably outside), lightly spray the interior and exterior of your can with an acrylic spray paint. Let dry thoroughly and apply a second coat. Let dry. Spray again with a spray sealant and let dry.

Step 3

Step 5: Place a bit of sand in the bottom of your new aluminarium to give it weight and to snuff out the flame, if necessary. Place a tea light in the aluminarium and enjoy. Betties always look better in candlelight.

Note: You can also punch the lid of an aluminum can to create a fun nightlight cover. Fold over the sharp edges with pliers and punch a couple of large holes at the top of your design. Affix to your nightlight with coated wire so it's a couple of inches away from the light source. Bend the wire so it wraps over the top of the nightlight.

NUTS & BOLTS NECKLACE

My dad bought me a toolbox a few years back, filling it with all sorts of mysterious stuff I've never figured out how or why to use. Since then, I've been using the box as a stepstool to get to my sweater shelf in the closet. Recently, I became curious so I took a deep breath, opened the toolbox, and repurposed those strange-looking stainless steel thingies by creating some funky industrial jewelry in just a few minutes.

You'll need:

- chain-nose pliers
- 3 1/2-inch key rings
- 3 stainless steel or brass nuts of varying sizes (find a small, a medium, and a large nut)
- 34-inch base metal ball chain and connector clasp

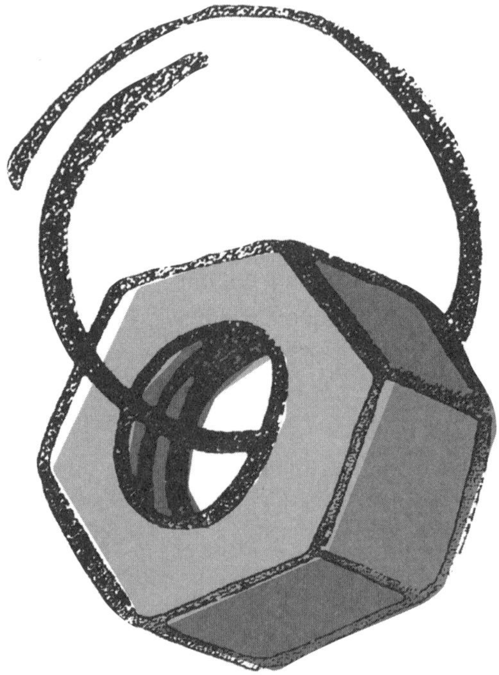

Step 1

Step 1: With chain-nose pliers, pry open one of the key rings and slip the small and medium nuts onto the ring. Pry open another key ring and slip the medium and large nuts onto the ring. Pry open the last jump ring and slip the large nut onto the ring.

Step 2: Slip the ball chain through the key ring that's attached to the large top nut. Add the connector clasp to each end of the ball chain and secure. Now the fun begins. You can wear this necklace in three ways: Long, slipped over your head; doubled, with the chain strung through the top key ring twice; and as a lariat, with the pendant end slipped through the folded end of the chain. Check yourself out in the mirror and admire how cool you are.

PAPER PETALS

I love surrounding myself with fresh flowers but I don't always have the coin to indulge my love of peonies, dahlias, and gerbera daisies. So during a one-person pity party, I raided my office supplies and whipped up some festive blooms, compliments of FedEx and the USPS.

Step 1

You'll need:

- 5 12 x $15\frac{1}{2}$ inch Tyvek envelopes
- compass and pencil
- sharp scissors
- 1 foot floral wire (or 20-gauge craft wire)
- 2 small 4-holed buttons
- floral tape

Step 1: On an envelope, use a compass to draw a circle with a radius of $2\frac{3}{4}$ inches (this will allow you to create a circle that doesn't hit the envelope's seam). Cut out two circles, one from each layer. Using one circle as a template, trace and cut out two more circles from this envelope, so that you are getting four circles from each envelope. Cut out circles from four more envelopes so you have a total of twenty circles.

Step 2: Fold the circles in half and snip two small diagonal cuts in the center, so you that you create one small diamond-shaped cut in the center of each circle.

Step 3: Fold a 12-inch piece of floral wire in half and thread a button onto the two prongs so that the button is snug in the fold of the wire. Press the two ends of the wire together and thread

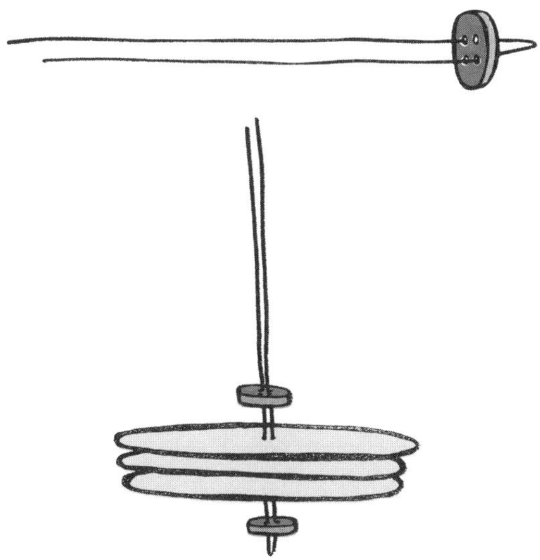

Step 3

the circles onto the wire. Slip each wire through a hole in another button and push it up until it's snug against the circles. Twist the wire around itself so that your flower is secure. Wrap floral tape around the floral wire to create a stem.

Step 4: With your scissors, make cuts around each circle, stopping short of the center. You are creating spiky petals. When you've finished, scrunch up the Tyvek petals with your hand to make your flower really bloom. Make a whole bouquet of these unexpected beauties—experiment with different sizes—and place them in a small vase.

Note: Thread a safety pin through a few of the bottom petals, clip the twisted wire, and wear your flower as a pin.

PET THE ROCK

I love stacking rocks when I'm communing with nature, and it always cheers me when I see cairns along trails or on tops of mountains. It makes me feel one with nature and one with my fellow Betties. My Bettilicious editor, Dana, suggested that I whip up a pile of felted "rocks." Brilliant idea, not that I would expect any less from her.

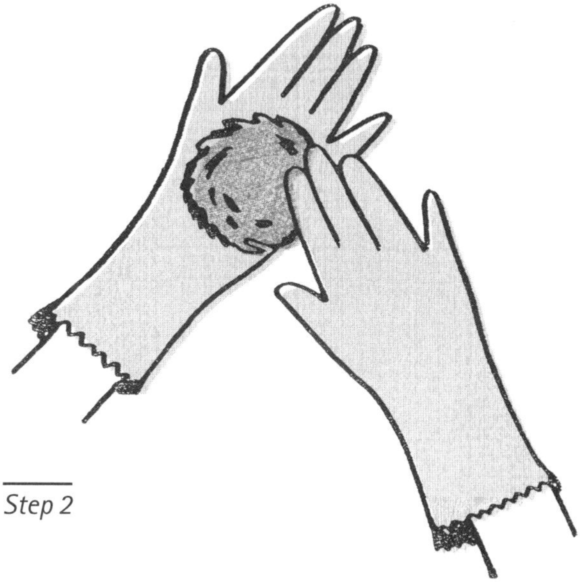

Step 2

You'll need:

- small plastic container with a lid
- hot water
- dishwashing liquid
- rubber gloves
- wool roving (combed unspun wool) in earthy colors (grey, brown, oatmeal)

Step 1: Fill a small plastic container with hot (almost boiling) water and a couple of drops of dishwashing liquid. Wearing rubber gloves, place a tuft of roving (start with a tuft that's about the size of two fingers) in the water and swish it around for several seconds. Remove it from the water and put the lid back on the container to keep the water hot.

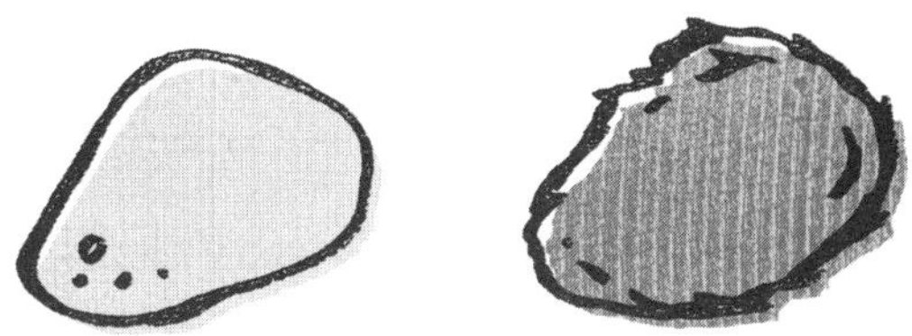

real rock   wool rock

Step 2: Gently roll the wool roving between your palms until it forms a ball. Continue rolling, periodically dipping the ball in the hot water and rolling some more. The wool will begin to full, becoming dense and taking on a round shape. Dip another tuft of roving in the water and drape it over your ball. Repeat your rolling technique until the new wool adheres to and becomes part of the ball. Keep adding roving to your ball and start shaping it in a flatter, rock-like shape. This may mean adding more roving to some areas of the ball. Your "rock" should start getting dense and solid—you don't want flyaway tufts on your rock. When your rock is the desired size, set it aside and let it dry.

Step 3: Create a couple more rocks and pebbles in the same manner, mixing up the size and shape. When you're done, stack them in a cairn and admire.

SHADOW BOXING

I dig shadow boxes, seeing as I like to collect things and often I don't have a surface on which to display them. My bookshelves are full. My tabletops are otherwise engaged. So when I bring home some treasures or I want to display my newest obsession (such as a magical ball of yarn) I need a shadow box to showcase my little beauties. Rather than running out to a giant craft store or that superstore with the bull's-eye logo, I whip up my own by sacrificing one of my tony shoe boxes.

You'll need:

- spray paint
- newspapers
- sturdy shoe box
- wrapping paper (on a roll, not folded)
- pencil
- sharp scissors
- spray mount
- adhesive Velcro

Step 1: Find an area outdoors and spread newspapers on the ground. Spray paint a shoe box, both inside and out. Let dry thoroughly. I used chocolate brown for a rich but neutral look.

Step 2: Place a sheet of wrapping paper wrong side up (I used a mod brown and baby blue paper). Place the box on the paper and trace around it with a pencil. With a sharp pair of scissors, cut out the paper. Check that it fits inside the back of the box. If not, trim it down. Spray the back of the wrapping paper with spray mount and fit it into the back of

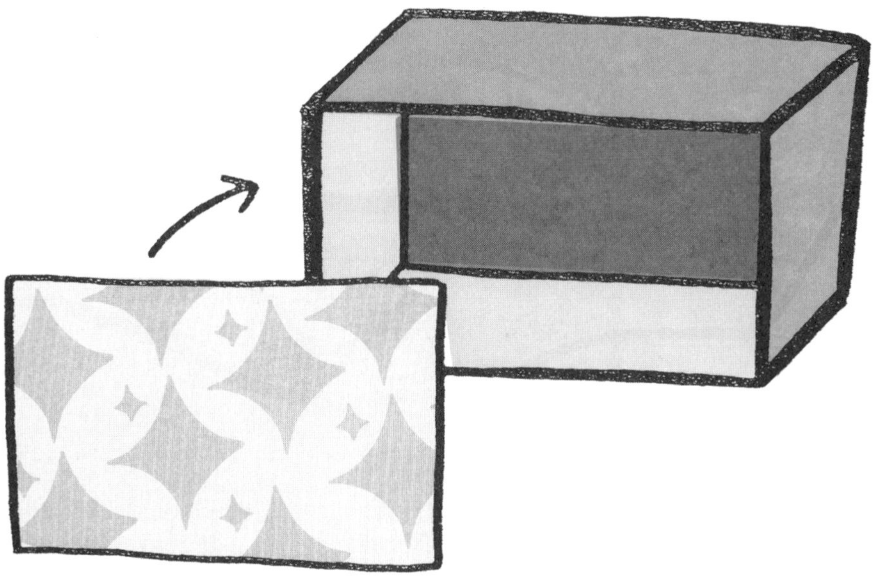

Step 2

your box. It's looking pretty sweet, isn't it?

Step 3: Cut out two pieces of adhesive Velcro and affix to the top two corners of your shadow box. Determine where you want to hang it and place the corresponding pieces of Velcro on the wall. Hang and proudly showcase your find of the month!

Note: If you want shelves inside your box, simply spray paint a smaller box and affix it with Velcro to the inside of the larger box.

PILLOW TALK

Grab that old sweater from a decade that shall not be named and transform it into a funky felted pillow. If that isn't enough, needle felt your initials on it so no one will try to make off with it during a particularly raucous party. Stuff it with shredded plastic bags to give them a new life, too.

You'll need:

- old wool sweater
- scissors
- straight pins
- wool yarn
- tapestry needle
- lingerie bag
- top-loading washing machine
- laundry detergent
- clean towel
- small plastic container with lid
- boiling water
- dishwashing liquid
- foam block
- wool roving
- 36-gauge felting needle
- loads of old plastic bags
- hand-sewing needle
- thread

Step 1: Pick out a pure wool sweater that you don't wear anymore but haven't gotten around to throwing out (or pick up an old sweater at a thrift store). A striped sweater is snazzy, but a solid sweater works well, too. Lay the sweater flat on a cutting mat or a wood floor. With sharp scissors, cut off the arms and the ribbing at the waist and neck. Now cut through both layers (the front and back of the sweater) to make two large squares or rectangles (one large piece from the front and one from the back). With right sides facing, pin the pieces together.

Step 1

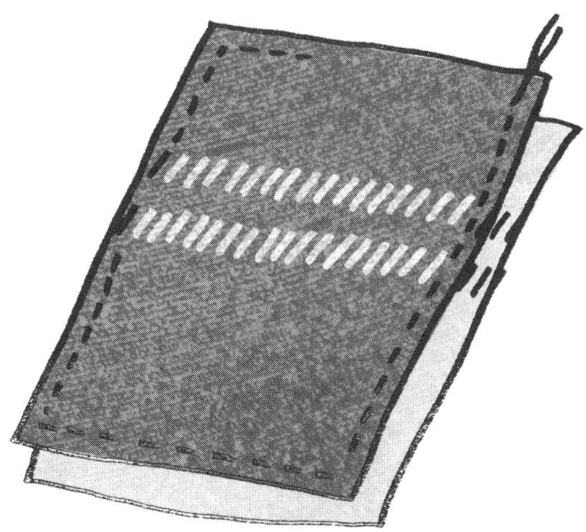

Step 2: Thread a long piece of yarn (the color doesn't matter really, as it won't show once felted) through a tapestry needle and, leaving a ½-inch seam allowance, backstitch (see page 19) around the perimeter, leaving a 6-inch opening at one of the ends. Turn your pillowcase right side out.

Step 3: Place the pillowcase in a lingerie bag and throw it in a top-loading washer. Set the water temperature to hot and the load to small. Add a normal amount of laundry detergent and let the machine get to agitating. Every few minutes, take out the lingerie bag and check the pillowcase. The hot water and agitation will shrink your wool and it will begin to full. Put it back in the machine if the stitches are still visible and the fabric still drapey. When the pillowcase gets to a denseness that you like, pull it out and rinse it in cold water. Place the pillowcase on a clean towel and gently roll the excess moisture out. Lay it flat to dry.

Step 4: It's time to dress up your pillowcase. Fill a small plastic container with boiling water and add a few drops of dishwashing liquid. Put the lid on until ready to use. Slip a foam block inside the case. Pull out a tuft of roving and dip it in the soapy hot water. Pull it apart so it's a long strand of fibers and position it where you want your initials or design to be (make sure the foam block is under the roving). With your felting needle, start stabbing the roving into place. Jab, jab, jab. The fibers will start to mesh with those of the pillowcase. Keep stabbing quickly and positioning the stray edges of the roving into place with the end of your needle as you go.

Step 4

Step 5

When this has felted, add more wet roving to the end of your first batch and keep stabbing and cleaning up the edges until you've completed your design. Admire your handiwork and let dry.

Step 5: With scissors, shred disposable plastic grocery bags. Stuff the pillowcase until it reaches a plumpness you like. With a needle and thread (yarn is too bulky for the felted fabric) in a complementary color, sew shut the pillow opening.

Note: Instead of adding your initials, add a pocket. With leftovers from the sweater, cut out a pocket shape and whipstitch it onto the front of the pillow before felting.

GREASY SPOON PLACEMATS

I order takeout more often than I'd like to admit. And I have wide-ranging tastes so the menus pile up in short order. I decided to take my menu surplus—at least the ones without huge grease stains on them—and transform them into cool placemats, perfect for takeout night (i.e. Tuesday, Thursday, and sometimes Sunday).

You'll need:

- scissors
- pile of old menus
- 4 sheets of 11 x 17 inch paper
- foam brush
- spray mount
- laminating machine

Step 1: With scissors, cut the menus into long strips . . . or however you like. If you have a lot of menus, you could cut out the restaurants' names and logos, your favorite items, whatever.

Step 2: On a piece of 11 x 17 paper, layer strips next to each other and slightly beyond the edge of the paper. Try to get as many different colors going on as possible. Once you've designed it to your satisfaction, spray the backs of your strips with spray mount and stick them in place. Set aside and let dry. Make three more placemats for a set of four. Trim the edges so the strips are flush with the edge of the backing sheet.

Step 1

Step 3: Take your placemat art to a copy shop that has a large laminating machine and run your sheets through the machine. With a small pair of scissors, trim the excess lamination off the placements and enjoy!

Note: You can make matching coasters using this same technique.

FOR THE RECORD BOWL

Every time I go home, I find some remnant of my childhood. Recently, I uncovered my much-loved Shaun Cassidy album. The problem was that I didn't have a turntable handy for my old vinyl. So I transformed my record into a bowl that I can use and enjoy on a daily basis. As for the album cover, I'm thinking about creating a shrine to Shaun.

You'll need:

- oven
- cookie sheet
- 9-inch metal bowl
- 33-RPM LP record
- pot holders

Step 1: Preheat your oven to 200°F. When the oven is heated, place the cookie sheet on a middle rack. Place the metal bowl upside down and center the record on top of the bowl. You might want to crack open a window or turn on your stove's hood fan for ventilation.

Step 2: After five minutes, remove the cookie sheet, bowl, and record. Using pot holders, flip the metal bowl so that it's upright. The record will now be pliable; place it in the bowl and shape it so that it becomes ruffled. Allow it to cool. Remove and enjoy!

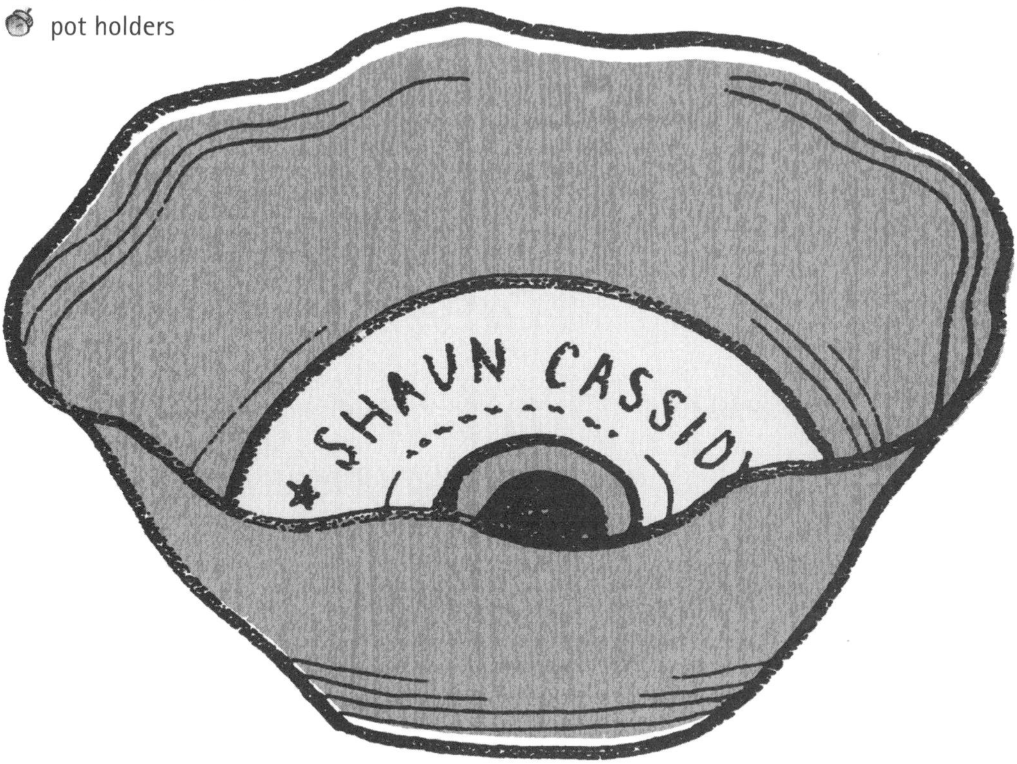

ADDITIONAL RESOURCES

In addition to my picks below, take time to stop and smell the craft opportunities. Check out flea markets, yard sales, estate sales, and thrift stores. Other people's junk could well be a key ingredient in your next work of art, or at least offer an extra stroke of genius.

WEBSITES AND BLOGS

Here are just a few of my favorite craft-related online resources.

Ace Hardware, www.acehardware.com: The place I head when I need hardware or tools. I can't craft any longer without my trusty Dremel tool. Ace *is* the place.

Angry Chicken, angrychicken.typepad.com: Seamstress Amy Karol is the force behind this great sewing site. I particularly dig her tutorials.

Candlescience, www.candlescience.com: My pal Emily steered me toward this site, which is geared toward crafty Betties looking to get started with waxes and wicks.

Craft Magazine, www.craftzine.com: For the indie crafting crowd, this is the place to hang out online. Chock full of news and tutorials, you'll find something new every time you log on.

CraftStylish, www.craftstylish.com: I love this terrific site, which features tutorials, news, and all sorts of inspiration for the omni-crafter.

Craftypod, www.craftypod.com: Diane Gilleland is a crafting guru and she shares all of her insight, secrets, and projects here. Her Craftypod podcast is also the bomb.

Etsy, www.etsy.com: This is my favorite crafty shopping site. When it's late at night and I have the jones to shop for unique, handmade items, this I where I head.

From Nature with Love, www.fromnaturewithlove.com: Purchase ingredients for body products and candles.

Home Depot, www.homedepot.com: A giant hardware resource.

How About Orange, www.howaboutorange.blogspot.com: This crafty blog by graphic designer Jessica Jones never fails to inspire me.

Joann Fabrics & Crafts, www.joann.com: Joann has been around for a long time and with good reason; it's a treasure trove for seamstresses (and crafters, too).

Knitty: Little Purls of Wisdom, www.knitty.com: This awesome site operates like an online magazine, with a host of new knitting projects published each season.

The Lamp Shop, www.lampshop.com: This site offers a great selection of lampshade frames.

Let It Shine Candle Supplies, www.letitshineusa.com: When you need large amounts of wax for candle-making, Let It Shine is the place to go.

Michaels, www.michaels.com: This is a great general craft resource.

Posie Gets Cosy, rosylittlethings.typepad.com: Alicia Paulson creates all sorts of lovely projects that are sweet, old-fashioned, and innovative.

Rockler Woodworking and Hardware, www.rockler.com: My Uncle Greg recommends this site for woodworking tools.

STORES

These are some of my favorite brick-and-mortar haunts in the Northwest and around the country.

Ballard Organics, 4759 Brooklyn Ave. NE, Seattle, WA 98105; (206) 527-2828; www.ballardorganics.com. Great source for organic essential oils and other supplies for body products.

Boersma's Sewing Center/Boersma's Knitting Basket, 203 NE 3rd St., McMinnville, OR 97128; (503) 472-4611; www.boersmas.com. These amazingly well-stocked shops are on neighboring corners in the charming town of McMinnville. The lower level of the sewing center houses a huge array of discount fabrics.

Bolt Fabric Boutique, 2136 NE Alberta St, Portland, OR 97211; (503) 287-2658; www.boltfabricboutique.com. This small but mighty shop features a well-edited selection of the newest and hippest fabrics and patterns.

Close Knit, 2140 NE Alberta St., Portland, OR 97211; (503) 288-4568; www.closeknitportland.com. Next to Bolt, Close Knit is a cozy shop chock full of scrumptious fibers.

Collage, 1639 NE Alberta St., Portland, OR 97211; (503) 804-2526; www.diylounge.com. Collage features a classroom space in the back for varied craft classes, while the store space features hard-to-find craft supplies such as laminating machines, wood-carving tools, and resins.

Fusion Beads, 3830 Stone Way N., Seattle, WA 98103; (206) 782-4595; www.fusionbeads.com. A well-stocked and well-designed store chock full of Swarovski, findings, seed beads, and semi-precious stones.

Hilltop Yarn, 2224 Queen Anne Ave. N., Seattle, WA 98109; (206) 282-1332; www.hilltopyarn.com. A cozy yarn shop in a restored Craftsman house on top of Queen Anne Hill.

Make Shop & Studio, 313 N. Bishop Ave., Dallas, TX 75208; (214) 256-3061; www.themakesite.com. A great combination of boutique and class space. Make offers classes for various crafts.

Nancy's Sewing Basket, 2221 Queen Anne Ave. N., Seattle, WA 98109; (206) 282-9112; www.nancyssewingbasket.com. Nancy's has a huge inventory and is the place to go for high-end fabrics and traditional tailoring supplies.

Pacific Fabrics and Crafts Outlet Store, 2230 4th Ave. S., Seattle, WA 98134; (206) 628-6237; www.pacificfabrics.com. Be still, my heart. This seamstress's mecca offers a huge array of every imaginable fabric.

Rosie's Yarn Cellar, 2017 Locust St., Philadelphia, PA; 19103; (215) 977-9276; www.rosiesyarncellar.com. Philly's jewelbox of a yarn shop, Rosie's is replete with yummy yarns and a knowledgeable staff.

The Quilting Loft, 2601 NW Market St., Seattle, WA 98107; (206) 706-0445; www.thequiltingloft.com. Where I really learned to sew, The Quilting Loft offers loads of classes in quilting and sewing, and is stocked to the brim with fabrics, including a large selection of batik.

Spool, 1912 South St., Philadelphia, PA 19146; (215) 545-0755; www.spoolsewing.com. A tiny fabric store, Spool features a drool-inducing array of hip fabrics and patterns and classroom space in the back.

BOOKS FOR BETTIES

Here are some terrific craft resources I have in my personal library. I'm always amazed and wowed by the gorgeous crafts and works of art others come up with. It makes me feel downright dull . . . but just for a second.

Berger, Shoshana, and Grace Hawthorne. *ReadyMade: How to Make [Almost] Everything: A Do-It-Yourself Primer.* New York: Clarkson Potter, 2005.

Blose, Nora, and Dawn Cusick. *Herb Drying Handbook.* Ashville, N.C.: Sterling/Lark, 1993.

Butler, Amy. *Amy Butler's In Stitches: More Than 25 Simple and Stylish Sewing Projects.* San Francisco: Chronicle Books, 2006.

Carson, Tsia. *Craftivitiy: 40 Projects for the DIY Lifestyle.* New York: Collins Living, 2006.

Hart, Jenny. *Sublime Stitching: Hundreds of Hip Embroidery Patterns and How-To.* San Francisco: Chronicle Books, 2006.

Jansdotter, Lotta. *Lotta Jansdotter's Simple Sewing: Patterns and How-To for 24 Fresh and Easy Projects.* San Francisco: Chronicle Books, 2007.

Jansdotter, Lotta. *Lotta Prints: How to Print with Anything, from Potatoes to Linoleum.* San Francisco: Chronicle Books, 2008.

Montano, Mark. *Big-Ass Book of Crafts.* New York: Simon Spotlight Entertainment, 2008.

Mullin, Wendy and Eviana Hartman, with Beci Orpin. *Sew U: The Built by Wendy Guide to Making Your Own Wardrobe.* New York: Bulfinch, 2006.

Peitzer, Bernice. *Forever Flowers: A Flower Lover's Guide to Selecting, Pressing, and Designing.* Iola, Wisc.: Krause Publications, 2000.

Radford, Leigh. *AlterKNITS: Imaginative Projects and Craftivity Exercises.* New York: STC Craft/Melanie Falick Books, 2005.

Rannels, Melissa, Melissa Alvarado, and Hope Meng. *Sew Subversive: Down and Dirty DIY for the Fabulous Fashionista.* Newtown, Conn.: Taunton Press, 2007.

Rannels, Melissa, Melissa Alvarado, and Hope Meng. *Subversive Seamster: Transform Thrift Store Threads into Street Couture.* Newtown, Conn.: Taunton Press, 2007.

Vitkus, Jessica. *AlternaCrafts: 20+ Hi-Style Lo-Budget Projects to Make.* New York: STC Craft/Melanie Falick Books, 2006.

MAGAZINES FOR CRAFTY BETTIES

Bead & Button, www.beadandbutton.com
BeadStyle, www.beadstylemag.com
Beadwork, www.interweave.com/bead/beadwork_magazine/
Bust, www.bust.com
Craft: Transforming Traditional Crafts, www.craftzine.com
Crafts 'n Things, www.craftsnthings.com
Craft Stylish, www.craftstylish.com
Interweave Knits, www.interweaveknits.com
Sew News, www.sewnews.com
Simply Beads, www.simplybeadsmagazine.com
Threads, www.taunton.com/threads
Vogue Knitting, www.vogueknitting.com
YMN: Yarn Market News, www.yarnmarketnews.com

LIST OF PROJECTS

INDEX